TECHNICAL REPORT

Improving the Energy Performance of Buildings

Learning from the European Union and Australia

Charles P. Ries, Joseph Jenkins, Oliver Wise

Supported by the Real Estate Roundtable and the Building Owners and Managers Association

RAND Environment, Energy, and Economic Development

A RAND INFRASTRUCTURE, SAFETY, AND ENVIRONMENT PROGRAM

This research was supported by the Real Estate Roundtable and the Building Owners and Managers Association and was conducted under the auspices of the Environment, Energy, and Economic Development Program (EEED) within RAND Infrastructure, Safety, and Environment (ISE).

Library of Congress Cataloging-in-Publication Data

Ries, Charles.
Improving the energy performance of buildings : learning from the European Union and Australia / Charles Ries, Joseph Jenkins, Oliver Wise.
p. cm.
ISBN 978-0-8330-4787-8 (pbk. : alk. paper)
1. Buildings—Energy conservation—European Union countries. 2. Buildings—Energy conservation—Australia. I. Jenkins, Joseph, 1985- II. Wise, Oliver. III. Title.

TJ163.5.B84R545 2009
333.79'62094—dc22

2009032283

Published 2009 by the RAND Corporation
1776 Main Street, P.O. Box 2138, Santa Monica, CA 90407-2138
1200 South Hayes Street, Arlington, VA 22202-5050
4570 Fifth Avenue, Suite 600, Pittsburgh, PA 15213-2665
RAND URL: http://www.rand.org/
To order RAND documents or to obtain additional information, contact
Distribution Services: Telephone: (310) 451-7002;
Fax: (310) 451-6915; Email: order@rand.org

Preface

In recent years, the European Union and its member nations and the Australian Commonwealth and some of its states and territories have pioneered policies to promote energy efficiency in buildings and to address market features that make energy efficiency difficult to achieve. This study examines how these policies have worked and draws implications for the design of similar public policies for the United States.

The study was undertaken by the RAND Corporation's Infrastructure, Safety, and Environment (ISE) Division, with support from the Real Estate Roundtable and the Building Owners and Managers Association, to aid American policymakers considering energy and carbon efficiency programs for commercial real estate in the United States. The findings are based on interviews of policymakers and stakeholders in the European Union and Australia and energy efficiency experts in the United States, as well as a review of relevant literature.

The report reviews building energy disclosure policies and "white-certificate" abatement programs in the European Union and Australia. The study did not include other possible policy instruments such as tax incentives, credit programs, or carbon taxation.

This study is part of RAND research on environmental issues and climate change. Recent publications include the following:

- *Impacts on U.S. Energy Expenditures and Greenhouse-Gas Emissions of Increasing Renewable Energy Use*, Michael Toman, James Griffin, and Robert J. Lempert (TR-384-1-EFC).
- *Evaluating Options for U.S. Greenhouse-Gas Mitigation Using Multiple Criteria,* Nicholas Burger, Liisa Ecola, Thomas Light, and Michael Toman (OP-252-RC).

The RAND Environment, Energy, and Economic Development Program

This research was conducted under the auspices of the Environment, Energy, and Economic Development Program (EEED) within RAND ISE. The mission of ISE is to improve the development, operation, use, and protection of society's essential physical assets and natural resources and to enhance the related social assets of safety and security of individuals in transit and in their workplaces and communities. The EEED research portfolio addresses environmental quality and regulation, energy resources and systems, water resources and systems, climate, natural hazards and disasters, and economic development—both domestically and internationally. EEED research is conducted for government, foundations, and the private sector.

Questions or comments about this report should be sent to the project leader, Charles Ries (ries@rand.org). Information about the Environment, Energy, and Economic Development Program is available online at www.rand.org/ise/environ. Inquiries about EEED projects should be sent to the Director, Keith Crane. He can be reached by email at kcrane@rand.org; by phone at 703-413-1100, ext. 5520; or by mail at The RAND Corporation, 1200 South Hayes Street, Arlington, VA 22202-5050.

More information about RAND is available at www.rand.org.

Contents

Figures

Summary

More than a third of the primary energy used in developed countries is used to heat, cool, and light buildings or is utilized within buildings. Studies by the Intergovernmental Panel on Climate Change (IPCC), McKinsey & Company, and other organizations have found that opportunities to achieve substantial, relatively low-cost improvements in energy efficiency can be found in commercial real estate.

However, the buildings sector has unique characteristics that make design of energy efficiency policies particularly challenging. For example, real estate purchases or leases are relatively infrequent because of high capital and transaction costs, and the variability of design and siting makes it inherently difficult to compare energy efficiency of buildings. As a result, potential renters, buyers, or investors often do not have enough information to make rational choices about energy efficiency investments. Also, the buildings industry is characterized by small-scale firms, which may not have the technical expertise necessary to make significant improvements in energy efficiency design or technology. Finally, there is a "split-incentive" problem when owners must bear the cost of energy efficiency improvements, but the benefits of their investment accrue to the tenant, who enjoys lower utility bills.

In recent years, the European Union (EU) and its member nations and the Australian Commonwealth and some of its states and territories have pioneered policies to promote energy efficiency in buildings and to address these market failures. This study examines how these policies have worked and draws implications for the design of similar public policies for the United States.

The EU has focused on disclosing information about the energy efficiency of buildings. Its Energy Performance in Buildings Directive (EPBD), issued in 2002 and implemented throughout the EU in 2009, requires that upon the sale or lease of any building or building unit, an energy performance certificate (EPC) must be presented to the prospective buyer or lessee. The certificates contain information on either the building or unit's energy efficiency *design* characteristics or its actual measured energy *usage*. The certificates are accompanied by benchmark values for comparable building types, to make them meaningful to users. As part of this system, EU member states have put in place inspection and rating systems and have made various decisions about the scope and content of certificates. The EPBD also requires that public buildings over a certain size have energy efficiency certificates posted in a prominent place where the general public can see them.

The EPBD is currently being adjusted in light of experience. The European Commission recently proposed amendments, because it believes the EPBD has been implemented inconsistently and additional energy efficiency gains can be made in the buildings sector.

These legislative efforts focus primarily on the energy used *by* a building in its standard operation (e.g., heating and cooling), not on energy used *within* a building by its occupants.

For example, the legislation might influence an owner to improve the performance of a new building by using better windows and insulation, but it would have no effect on the energy consumption of a tenant operating a restaurant with industrial ovens and refrigerators, because, absent "green leases" or other tenant energy-use tracking, tenants have little incentive (beyond minimizing their utility bills) to make investments to improve energy performance. This is a significant point, as the energy used by occupants typically accounts for a large percentage of the total energy used at a building site.

In Australia, a national program for rating the energy of residential buildings has been in place for several years, alongside voluntary rating systems similar to those used in the United States. Additionally, the states of New South Wales and Victoria have experimented with policies that allow building owners and other energy users to earn abatement certificates ("white certificates") by installing specific types of equipment or fixtures that improve energy efficiency. Recently, similar white-certificate programs have been rolled out in France and Italy. In France, the vast majority of certificates have been earned by residential building owners. In Australia, as in the EU, policies are being revised.

Energy Efficiency Issues

Public policies in the EU and Australia to promote building energy efficiency have addressed many of the same issues. These include

- Building codes
- Energy efficiency certificates
- Promoting energy efficiency in public buildings
- Training and certification of experts
- White-certificate programs.

Building Codes

Building codes have been effective in improving energy efficiency in new buildings and in some buildings undergoing major refurbishments, because they are mandatory and generally quite specific about requirements. As a public policy tool, however, codes are slow to have an aggregate effect on energy use, because even in years of healthy economic growth, only about 3 percent of a nation's building stock is newly built or renovated. The EU now requires all member countries to have energy efficiency elements in building codes, and the codes must be reviewed every five years (although there is no affirmative obligation to update them on review). Whether codes should be prescriptive or performance-based is a major decision. Most codes are highly prescriptive, which reduces inspection costs and allows building-materials manufacturers to standardize. The downside of prescriptive codes is that they can inhibit design innovation. Performance-based codes for energy efficiency are less common. Although such codes can inspire new design approaches, such as the use of building siting, passive features, and other non-materials-based efficiency improvements, they require more highly trained inspectors to certify compliance. Energy efficiency compliance with building codes often can be certified at the same time as other requirements, which reduces implementation costs. In some jurisdictions, particularly EU countries that are new users of building codes, compliance with code requirements is an issue. In Bulgaria, a national energy efficiency agency has been established, partly to ensure compliance with energy aspects of building codes.

Certificates

The requirement to present a standardized rating of a building's energy characteristics before or at the time of sale or lease is a central aspect of the EU's approach. Some Australian states and the Australian Capital Territory (which comprises the national capital Canberra and its environs) also require energy efficiency certificates. It is assumed that buyers and sellers (or lessees and lessors) thus informed will value good energy performance. However, energy efficiency information is most effective if it is provided before the transaction, since at the time of transaction, most issues, including price, have already been agreed on, so the effect of energy efficiency information on decisions is lessened. For this reason, the European Commission in November 2008 proposed amending the EPBD to require energy ratings to be disclosed when properties are listed or advertised.

The ratings on energy efficiency certificates may be based on a building's design characteristics (asset rating) or measured energy performance (operational rating) or—as some jurisdictions have sought—both. The EU leaves this decision to the discretion of member states. A design-based approach is often the only alternative for new construction, and it facilitates cross-building comparisons by potential buyers and renters. It also recognizes that, in principle, many building owners have no control over tenant behavior (unless "green leases" are used). In contrast, energy-usage-based ratings convey information about the building or unit's measured energy use, can be prepared by a utility, and may be audited. However, in multitenant buildings, energy usage is mainly determined by tenant behavior, and tenants may not have an interest in the building's rating.

The use of benchmark buildings or standardized rating categories simplifies the comparison of ratings for consumers. However, incentives may be needed to improve the energy efficiency of older, poorly performing buildings. In many instances, making older buildings more efficient can achieve the greatest improvements in energy efficiency, but when the standards for the highest ratings are based on the most efficient new buildings, owners of older buildings may not be able to attain them, even with extensive renovation. The owners of such older buildings may therefore see little economic return at sale or rental from investments in improving energy efficiency.

Promoting Energy Efficiency in Public Buildings

The EU applies special disclosure obligations to "public buildings" that have more than 1,000 sq m of useful floor area. Member states can decide what qualifies as "public." Although a few have written the definition broadly (to include, for example, malls or hospitals that are generally open to the public), most apply the requirements only to buildings owned or occupied by government entities. However "public" is defined, the EU requires that such buildings post display energy certificates (DECs) in a prominent place to inform visitors and occupants of the buildings' energy efficiency ratings. In Australia, several jurisdictions have policies that set a minimum "Green Star" voluntary rating for any building that is leased or purchased for government use. The market power of the state governments in Victoria and New South Wales (where an estimated 40 percent of the floor space in the central business district is leased to public entities) is such that these policies are said to establish a de facto minimum for new speculative office-space construction.

A requirement to display energy certificates in prominent places (where voters can see them) can serve as an incentive for public authorities to invest in energy efficiency for publicly owned or leased buildings. Yet some jurisdictions in Europe (particularly subnational jurisdictions) have resisted appraising and rating public buildings, because of the potentially significant costs involved, even before the cost of energy efficiency improvements is considered. Objective disclosure in ubiquitous public structures such as schools, post offices, and public-service offices could garner public support and understanding for improvement programs. Since public buildings are normally under the control of public authorities, it would generally be preferable to have the energy certificates of those buildings based on actual energy usage rather than on design criteria, or to include both indicators.

Training and Certification of Experts

The credibility and effectiveness of public policies to improve energy efficiency in buildings in the EU and Australia depend primarily on the quality and impartiality of the experts who review the designs, inspect completed buildings, and issue ratings certificates. Design or usage ratings should ideally be based on a case-by-case review of designs or as-built structures. Ratings can confer substantial market value to buildings—or can decrease value. It is therefore necessary to carefully train and certify a large number of experts to determine energy performance ratings and support white-certificate programs. The largest number of inspectors is generally needed at the initiation of a program, before a building is certified.

A shortage of trained experts led the EU to postpone the entry in force of the EPBD for three years. The European Commission's proposed amendments will require member states to put in place quality-assurance programs to maintain the credibility of the system. Roughly half of the EU member states allow inspectors to be employees of interested parties (e.g., building design firms or developers).

White-Certificate Programs

White certificates are tradable rights based on specified energy efficiency investments, such as investments in improving the energy efficiency of buildings. White-certificate programs have been instituted as part of energy efficiency and cap-and-trade programs in some Australian states and also in Italy and France. Two key challenges for white-certificate programs relate to the definition of "business as usual": (1) determining the reduction in energy use to be imposed on an obligated party (typically a utility), and (2) verifying the consumer behavior that qualifies for certificate rights.

In New South Wales, Australia, under a white-certificate program aimed at carbon emissions, certificates could be earned by installing specified high-efficiency equipment. However, most of the certificates were in fact earned by firms that distributed low-cost equipment that improved energy efficiency (typically compact fluorescent bulbs and low-flow shower heads) to residential building owners. Such third-party aggregators sold corresponding white certificates to the utilities and large industrial users. Subsequent studies found a mixed record in installation of the equipment, and the program has ended. As a public policy approach to energy efficiency in buildings, white-certificate programs can provide incentives, but their effectiveness depends on the rigor of the efficiency gains required and the system of verification and enforcement.

One Australian group is proposing adoption of a buildings-only white-certificate program in which building owners can meet efficiency improvement obligations by investing in energy savings or by purchasing white certificates from other buildings that can achieve better-than-required energy savings.

Assessment of Program Impacts

The EU and Australian policies reviewed in this study are too new to permit definitive assessments of their impact. Moreover, it is difficult to disaggregate the effects of aspects of public policies that are customarily implemented in bundles (i.e., with pricing, tax incentives, and other components). One study of residential building transactions in Denmark found no statistical relationship between energy use by households and the presentation of EPCs at sale. In contrast, a study in the Australian Capital Territory found a significant correlation between house energy rating and sales price, after controlling for other factors. A study of the office-building market in the United States found a significant relationship between average achieved rental income and vacancy rates of buildings that have (voluntary) energy efficiency design and that use energy ratings and those of comparable buildings in close proximity. However, more research is required to assess accurately the cost-effectiveness of policies to improve energy efficiency in buildings.

Lessons for the United States

The experiences of Europe and Australia suggest that effective policies to promote energy efficiency in buildings can be designed using information disclosure, building codes, financial incentives, and benchmarking. The rollout of such policies and their consistent implementation pose special challenges. Our preliminary review of the European and Australian record suggests that the following key insights should be taken into account as the United States considers analogous policy approaches:

- **Codes.** In the near term, at least regional (climatic zone) consistency in the energy efficiency requirements for building codes would be highly desirable. This would allow building-materials manufacturers to improve and standardize building components. Given the importance of tenant behavior in energy consumption, consideration should also be given to applying energy efficiency code requirements to tenant interior space adaptations, especially in office and retail buildings. For the longer term, performance codes should be considered, but in the short term, simpler-to-administer prescriptive codes are preferable. Any expanded use of building codes should be accompanied by aggressive training and quality-assurance programs for inspectors.
- **Certificates.** An information mechanism such as EPCs needs to be simple enough to be understandable yet meaningful enough to affect marketplace behavior. Benchmarking can help, but the enormous variety of building types and siting makes establishment of reference grades very challenging. Once benchmark values are established, allowing (or, even better, requiring) them to be used in property advertisements and listings seems preferable to requiring declarations at the time of settlement. Building owners should also be allowed to display certificates at their option.

- **Attention to the incentives for improvements to existing buildings.** While public policies (especially codes) can affect the energy performance of newly built structures, widespread energy efficiency gains can be achieved only through retrofitting and making operational improvements to existing buildings. Management improvements are easier, cheaper, and faster to make than capital improvements, and benchmarks are an imperfect instrument for encouraging such improvements. Energy usage monitoring and incentives, marketable "white" abatement certificates, inspection, and improvement-recommendation systems will be essential for this effort.
- **Public buildings.** Public buildings should continue to be a test bed for new energy-saving ideas and should promote awareness of building energy performance levels. Nationwide standards for disclosure of energy performance of public buildings can serve both objectives. Given public sector control of most public building operations, disclosure usually should be based on measured energy usage, with an option to provide design ratings, where they exist.
- **Training and certification of experts.** The credibility of any building energy efficiency program depends on the quality and impartiality of the experts who review designs and usage data. No certificate or rating program should be started until an adequate supply of trained and licensed inspectors is on hand. National standards for training and certification could reduce the burden on states.
- **White certificates.** Building energy efficiency programs, with their large potential gains, can play an important part of a carbon (or energy use) cap-and-trade program. The challenge will be to accurately evaluate energy performance improvements and to ensure the credibility of the certificates in a sector with so many actors. It would be more difficult for utilities in the United States to play the role of aggregator and verifier than it would be for those in a country such as Australia, which has state-owned electricity monopolies. Establishment of a system of buildings efficiency ratings and the availability of a cadre of trained and licensed experts to implement it thus would seem to be preconditions for rollout of any broad-based white-certificate program in the United States.
- **Encouragement of voluntary measures.** There are a variety of voluntary initiatives in the buildings energy field, including voluntary rating schemes (such as ENERGY STAR; the U.S. Green Building Council's Leadership in Energy and Environmental Design (LEED); and the UK's Building Research Establishment Environmental Assessment Method (BREEAM)), "green leases" (in the UK and Australia), and tenant energy statements (in the UK). National policy should continue to encourage these schemes, as they can pioneer new approaches and front-load the development energy evaluation expertise in the private sector.
- **Monitoring and evaluation.** Supporting public policy approaches to increasing efficiency in this varied, but important sector will require effective monitoring and evaluation systems. Consideration should be given to increasing the building energy use research budgets of the Environmental Protection Agency and the Department of Energy.

Acronyms

BASIX	Buildings Sustainability Index
BCA	Building Code of Australia
BREEAM	Building Research Establishment Environmental Assessment Method
CEN	European Committee for Standardization
CFL	compact fluorescent light bulb
COAG	Council of Australian Governments
DEC	display energy certificate
EER	energy efficiency rating
EIA	Energy Information Administration
EPA	Environmental Protection Agency
EPBD	Energy Performance of Buildings Directive
EPC	energy performance certificate
ETS	Energy Efficiency Trading Scheme
EU	European Union
GGAS	Greenhouse Gas Abatement Scheme
HVAC	heating, ventilating, and air-conditioning
IPCC	Intergovernmental Panel on Climate Change
LEED	Leadership in Energy and Environmental Design
NABERS	National Australian Built Environment Rating System
NEET	New South Wales Energy Efficiency Trading Scheme
NGAC	New South Wales Greenhouse Gas Abatement Certificate
NGO	non-governmental organization
R&D	research and development
SAVE	Specific Actions for Vigorous Energy Efficiency
UK	United Kingdom
VEET	Victorian Energy Efficiency Target Scheme

CHAPTER ONE

Introduction

Total Global and U.S. Energy Demand

Commercial building space[1] accounts for about 18 percent of all energy consumption in the United States and is the fastest growing sector in end-use consumption (Alliance to Save Energy, 2008). From 1950 to 2006, end-use energy consumption by commercial buildings grew by 2.8 percent each year. This growth was a consequence of two developments: (1) increases in the stock of commercial buildings, and (2) shifts away from natural gas or other primary fuels toward electricity and the accompanying system energy losses (Andrews and Krogmann, 2009). Another trend affecting electricity consumption within buildings was the increasing use of electrical equipment, often left "on" or in standby mode 24/7.

No single type of space defines commercial buildings. Commercial space is used primarily for offices, retail, warehouse and storage, and education (Energy Information Administration, 2008, Table A1). Energy usage in commercial space tends to be greatest by providers of some type of service (e.g., food service, inpatient health care, food sales) (Energy Information Administration, 2008, Table C3). Figure 1.1 shows overall energy consumption by various types of commercial buildings in the United States in 2003.

Figure 1.2 shows that about half of all commercial energy end-use, weighed by carbon-dioxide emissions, is in lighting (25 percent), space cooling (13 percent), and space heating (12 percent). Each of these areas offers opportunity for significant reductions in energy use through advances in building technology and energy efficiency in heating and cooling.

Globally, energy demand in the commercial buildings sector is expected to grow by 2.2 percent annually through 2030 (McKinsey Global Institute, 2007). This growth will be driven primarily by increases in commercial floor space, which is projected to grow by 3 percent each year in the developing world, increasing at a slower rate in developed nations such as the United States (1.7 percent) (McKinsey Global Institute, 2007). Building use, occupant use patterns, and appliances are also driving factors in energy demand.

Opportunities for Improving Energy Efficiency in Buildings

A 2007 McKinsey & Company analysis found that the largest potential reductions in carbon-dioxide emissions at costs below $50 per ton of carbon dioxide emitted are in the power sector (27 percent), followed closely by the buildings sector (24 percent). The remainder is dispersed

[1] The U.S. Energy Information Administration (EIA) defines commercial buildings as buildings that are neither residential (single-family or multifamily), manufacturing/industrial, nor agricultural.

Figure 1.1
Energy Consumption of Commercial Buildings in the United States (2003)

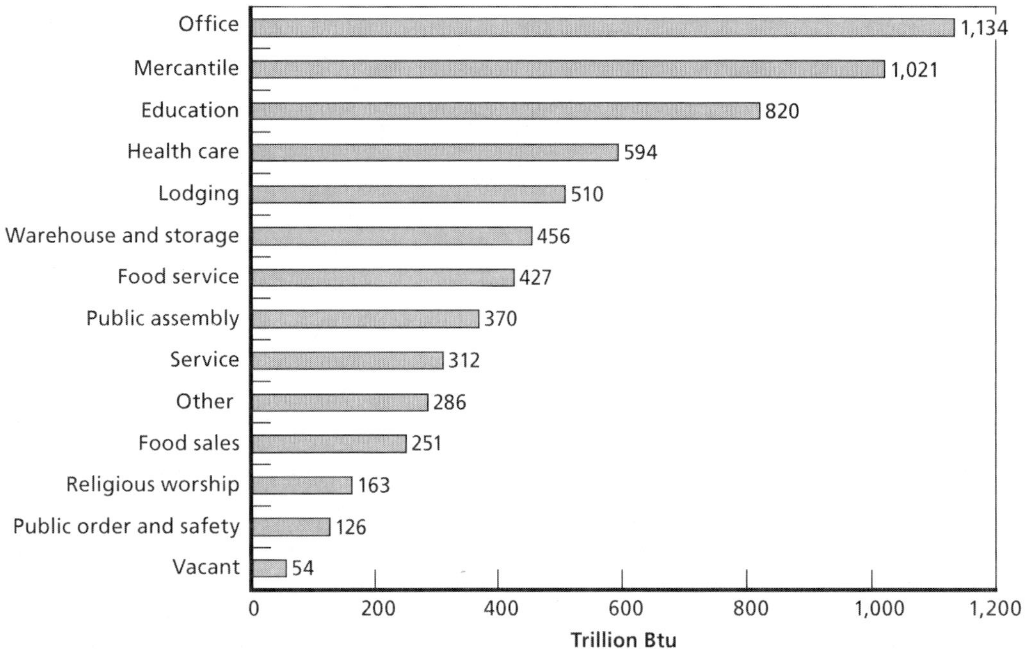

SOURCE: Energy Information Administration, 2003, Table A1.
RAND *TR728-1.1*

among the industrial, transportation, forestry, agricultural, and waste sectors (Creyts et al., 2007). The McKinsey study argues that a number of improvements in energy efficiency in buildings have a high social rate of return—in some cases, building owners or operators can recoup their investment in a reasonable period of time, and in others, the society as a whole would benefit, even though split incentives (i.e., when building owners must pay for energy efficiency improvements, but the benefits of their investment accrue to the tenant who enjoys lower utility bills) prevent building owners or tenants from achieving economic rates of return individually. The buildings sector has unique characteristics that make design of energy efficiency programs particularly challenging. Real estate purchases or leases are relatively infrequent, because of high capital and transaction costs. In addition, the variability of design and siting makes it inherently difficult to compare energy efficiency of buildings. As a result, potential renters, buyers, or investors often do not have enough information to make rational investment choices. Finally, the buildings industry is characterized by small-scale firms, which often lack the technical expertise necessary to make significant improvements in energy efficiency design or technology (Organisation for Economic Co-operation and Development, 2002b).

The McKinsey analysis concluded, however, that if these barriers could be overcome, 40 percent of the currently proposed measures to reduce emissions of carbon dioxide from buildings would more than cover the costs over the life of the improvements (Creyts et al., 2007).

While many energy efficiency improvements are self-financing, it can take as much as 30 years to reap the payoff. Improvements often require large up-front investments, which may present a barrier to building owners. Options for getting over this barrier include grants, tax

Figure 1.2
Commercial Energy End-Use Carbon-Dioxide Emissions in the United States

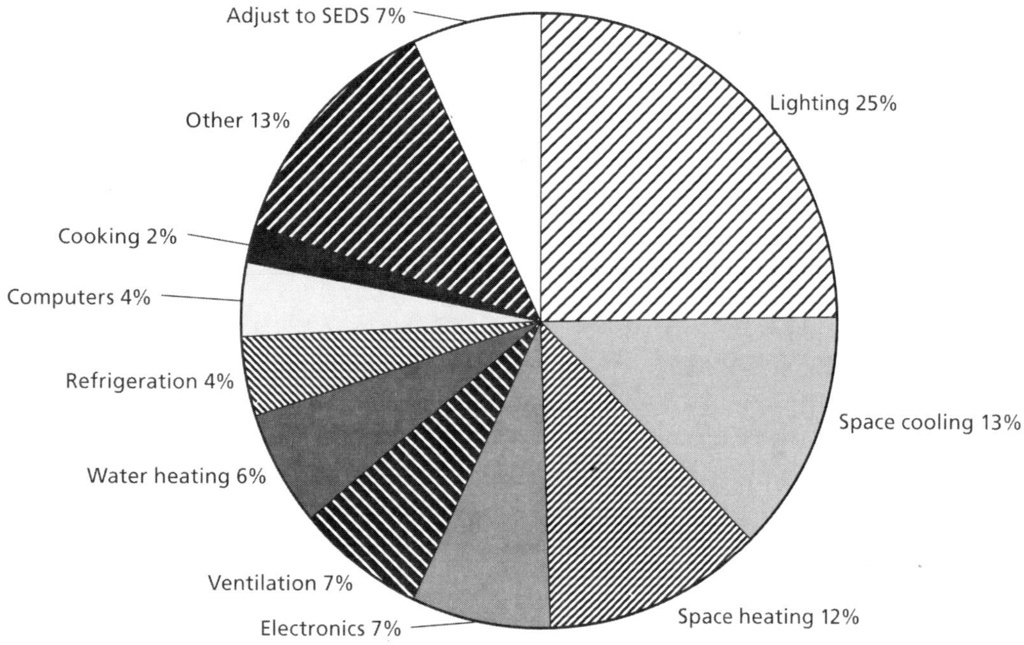

SOURCE: U.S. Department of Energy, 2008, Table 3.1.4.
NOTE: SEDS = State Energy Data System.
RAND *TR728-1.2*

credits for energy improvements, and "green" depreciation, which allows owners to use accelerated depreciation rates and defer tax payments (Australian Sustainable Built Environment Council, n.d.).

Investments in energy efficiency offer other benefits beyond cost savings. The "green job" market is projected to be one of the fastest growing sectors in the future. A European Commission study estimated that the effort to cut energy consumption by 20 percent by 2020 would lead to the creation of up to 1 million new jobs in refurbishment, alternative fuels, and other activities (European Commission, 2005). Other benefits include improved health for occupants of energy efficient buildings and productivity increases resulting from more fresh air flow for workers (Fisk, 2000).

Options for Improving Buildings Sector Efficiency

Very aggressive adoption of measures to improve energy efficiency in commercial buildings—for example, design changes that harness passive solar heating and daylight—has reduced energy consumption in some buildings by 50 to 75 percent (Levine et al., 2007).

Energy efficiency improvements in buildings are of three types: better control and management of energy use, better designs for new construction, and retrofits to existing buildings. Control and management improvements seldom require large up-front investments and can yield substantial savings.[2] Retrofitting a building is usually more expensive than incorporating energy efficient designs, insulation, materials, and technologies into new buildings. However, to emphasize only new construction would neglect substantial potential reductions in energy use in existing buildings, reductions that will be needed to reduce overall energy use by commercial real estate. Over the coming decades, the more than 72 billion sq ft of existing U.S. commercial building space (Energy Information Administration, 2008, Table A1) will account for the lion's share of energy consumption from this sector. Areas in which potential reductions in energy use could be realized include the thermal envelope, lighting, and climate control.

Thermal Envelope

Transfer of heat from the exterior to the interior of climate-controlled spaces and vice versa results in a significant loss of energy. Thus, improvements to the thermal envelope of a building can produce large savings. Enhancements may include improvements in installation, capitalizing on advances in the efficiency of windows and doors, improving the exchange of heat, and increasing the tightness of the building envelope. Improvements to the thermal envelope of a building can reduce heating loads by more than 30 percent (Levine et al., 2007; Demirbilek et al., 2000). Similarly, advances in window technology, such as improved glazing, can reduce the intake of passive solar heat by 75 percent and thus reduce cooling needs (Levine et al., 2007).

Lighting

A recent Intergovernmental Panel on Climate Change (IPCC) study found that through the prudent use of overhead lighting—e.g., use of more energy efficient lights, daylight, and dimmer sensors to control lights based on occupancy—daylight energy use can be cut by 75 to 90 percent (Levine et al., 2007). This is a significant savings, since lighting constitutes 25 percent of U.S. commercial energy end-use (U.S. Department of Energy, 2008, Table 3.1.4). Today, much of the lighting in public spaces does not use energy-saving options such as more efficient lighting devices, daylight, reflective wall and floor coverings, or tailored lighting choices (Levine et al., 2007). Studies have found that using daylight at the perimeter of office buildings can reduce light consumption by 40 to 80 percent (Levine et al., 2007). Many lighting improvements, including light-emitting diodes and compact fluorescent light bulbs (CFLs), could more than pay for themselves through reductions in energy use (Creyts et al., 2007).

Climate Control

More efficient heating and cooling choices also offer opportunities for energy savings. Efficiency gains can be made by using improved equipment and also by ensuring that existing systems are correctly installed and operated. Energy audits can identify efficiency gains made possible by upgrades or improvements in maintenance (Creyts et al., 2007). Finally, combined heat and power units could improve energy efficiency, although they are typically suitable only for very large buildings or complexes or for municipalities.

---

[2] One United Kingdom (UK) energy consultant noted that energy savings of 20 percent or more can be achieved in commercial buildings, particularly when unnecessary 24/7 operations are curtailed (e-mail exchange, June 27, 2009).

Barriers to Demand Reduction

A variety of barriers have discouraged the adoption of measures to improve energy efficiency in commercial buildings. These barriers include lack of information, split incentives, and financial disincentives.

Lack of Information

Lack of information about available energy efficiency options is a major barrier to the adoption of new technologies. Although building owners and operators are usually aware that new products and procedures will save energy, few realize how much energy can be saved and how cost-effective certain improvements can be. To overcome this barrier, many countries in Europe are requiring building owners to disclose energy performance during building transactions and are also launching aggressive public advertising campaigns to raise awareness.

Split Incentives

In commercial buildings and non-owner-occupied residential buildings, tenants often pay for the energy consumed. Owners who do not pay these costs may be reluctant to invest in improving energy efficiency, because they are not sure they can recoup the costs by charging higher rents.[3]

Financial Disincentives

The need for large up-front capital investment can be another barrier to improving energy efficiency. While property owners may know that they can realize substantial savings over the long run, the initial investment may be so high that they have difficulty financing it. Alternatively, owners may be uncertain that they can recoup the investment if they sell the buildings, because the market does not value the investment appropriately. Some property companies may not invest in reducing energy consumption because the rate of return on the energy efficiency investment, while positive and correctly assessed, is not as attractive as prospective returns on alternative investments. But to the extent that energy is not priced to fully reflect social costs, the rate of return to efficiency improvements can be considered artificially low, creating a market failure.

Policy Options for Overcoming Barriers

Governments that wish to induce property companies to invest more heavily in reducing energy consumption may employ a variety of policy options. Koomey et al. (2001) identified six broad categories of policy options for the commercial buildings sector:

1. Equipment standards
2. Building codes
3. Voluntary programs
4. State/utility programs

[3] A recent study, however, found that in the U.S. office-building market, buildings certified as energy efficient do command higher rents and have higher occupancy rates.

5. Tax credits
6. Support for research and development (R&D) to improve energy efficiency.

Koomey et al. argue that equipment standards, voluntary programs, and R&D play a lead role in saving energy, while building codes, tax credits, and state/utility programs are useful but somewhat less beneficial.

Recent efforts to improve building energy performance have focused on the certification of buildings. Some of these programs, such as the U.S. Green Building Council's Leadership in Energy and Environmental Design (LEED), are managed by private organizations, while others are administered by government agencies such as the U.S. Environmental Protection Agency (EPA). Most of the U.S. programs, including LEED and EPA's ENERGY STAR, are voluntary, while the European Union's (EU's) Energy Performance of Buildings Directive (EPBD) is mandatory for certain classes of buildings. Voluntary and mandatory rating systems have different characteristics. Voluntary ratings can be selectively administered (e.g., "We cannot rate you unless . . ."), can be relatively expensive, and can be somewhat subjective. Mandatory rating systems must be inexpensive, robust, and replicable.[4]

The LEED program is designed to encourage and recognize buildings that exceed building-code energy efficiency and sustainability standards. It awards points in six categories:

1. Sustainable sites
2. Water efficiency
3. Energy and atmosphere
4. Materials and resources
5. Indoor environmental quality
6. Innovation and design processes.

Buildings awarded a LEED minimum threshold point count can receive a rating of certified; higher point counts can achieve ratings up to platinum.

The ENERGY STAR program for buildings and manufacturing plants provides a free rating tool, called Portfolio Manager, that owners and managers can use to determine their total energy use and benchmark their buildings against other buildings of similar type and size. ENERGY STAR gives buildings scores of from 0 to 100 and awards an ENERGY STAR plaque to the top 25 percent of them. ENERGY STAR is geared toward building operation; it focuses on helping owners understand how their building compares with similar buildings and where there is room for improvement.

---

[4] Email from UK energy consultant, June 27, 2009.

CHAPTER TWO

European Approaches

Early Approaches

Early European energy security efforts focused on increasing Europe's energy supply, not on moderating demand for energy (David, 2007). After Denmark joined the European Economic Community[1] in 1973, this focus began to change. Denmark brought with it a different set of ideas based on an energy policy of controlling demand (David, 2007). Prior to its first rotation as President of the Council of Ministers, Denmark began advocating a demand-based approach to European energy policy.

The first fruit of this approach was a proposal for a directive on a system for energy audits of EU buildings in 1987 (David, 2007). The proposal did not receive widespread support. It did, however, lead to the Specific Actions for Vigorous Energy Efficiency (SAVE) directive two years later, in 1989. This directive marked the beginning of a new era in which the European Commission was interested not only in energy policy but also in environmental policy (David, 2007). The version of SAVE finally implemented in 1993 introduced six ideas relevant to the buildings sector which would later become part of the EPBD:

- Energy certification of buildings
- Separate billing for heating, hot water, and air-conditioning, based on actual consumption
- Third-party financing for energy savings in the public sector
- The need for thermal insulation of buildings
- Inspection of boilers
- Energy audits in big industrial installations.

As concern over climate change and greenhouse-gas emissions mounted, the EU made a commitment at the United Nations Framework Convention on Climate Change in Kyoto to reduce its emissions of carbon dioxide by 8 percent from a 1990 baseline by 2010. This commitment sparked discussion over how Europe would meet its obligation, resulting in the Action Plan to Improve Energy Efficiency in the European Community, which was adopted in 2000 (a revised version was issued in 2006). The plan proposed reinforcing existing energy programs and implementing new ones. It suggested that a 1 percent reduction in energy use per year was possible (Commission of the European Communities, 2000).

[1] Pursuant to treaty changes, the institution was later renamed the European Community and now is the EU.

Energy Performance of Buildings Directive

In 2001, a proposal was put forth to improve the impact of the SAVE directive by "[laying] down more concrete actions with a view to achieving the great unrealised potential for energy savings and reducing the large differences between Member States' results in the buildings sector" (European Commission, 2002). This proposal would ultimately become the EPBD, which was passed in December 2002. The justification for the EPBD was the twin goals of decreasing Europe's dependence on foreign sources of energy and thus improving energy security and decreasing emissions of carbon dioxide.

The EPBD comprises five major themes:

1. Certification of buildings
2. Inspection of boilers
3. Inspection of air-conditioning systems
4. Methodologies for calculating the energy performance of buildings
5. Implementation of minimum energy performance requirements for new buildings and for major renovations.

A deadline of January 4, 2006, was set for member states to transpose the EPBD into national legislation. This deadline was subsequently extended to January 1, 2009, because member states found themselves unable to put the required number of certification experts in place in time to meet the original date. As of January 2009, 22 of 27 member states had fully complied with the directive.

The EU principle of subsidiarity dictates that, if possible, legislation should be handled at the national level rather than being dictated to member states. As a result, the EPBD only outlines broad guidelines and leaves most of the details up to member states as they transpose the directive into national law. Not surprisingly, there is great disparity among member states in implementation approaches and levels of ambition.

Certification of Buildings

The EPBD requires member states to implement a program of energy performance certificates (EPCs) for both new and existing buildings. The EPCs, which are valid for 10 years, are to be issued when new buildings are constructed and made available to purchasers or tenants at the point of sale or lease of buildings. The EPBD affords member states autonomy to design the certificates and establish grading standards. Member states have almost universally made use of the A–G rating scale already in use for energy ratings on European appliances. Although the European Committee for Standardization (CEN) began development of standards (e.g., for asset and operational ratings) to support the directive, they were not available as member states were developing national legislation. Thus, considerable disparities in details emerged.[2] Because of differences in calculation procedures and benchmarks across countries, a rating of B in one member state may not signify the same energy efficiency performance level as a B in another state.

---

[2] Among the 30 or so CEN standards that were written or amended to support the EPBD, European Standard EN15603 defined the energy ratings used in EPCs and EN15217 defined how they could be expressed (e-mail exchange with UK energy consultant, June 27, 2009).

Certificates also differ in the types of information they display. The EU member states have weighed the trade-off between offering detailed information and potentially overwhelming the people the certificates are intended to inform, and most have come down on the side of simplicity. Most have also chosen to require the certificates to contain a series of tailored recommendations that would, if implemented, improve energy performance. These recommendations are generally optional. However, Denmark and Portugal are requiring public buildings to implement some of them. Denmark gives owners of public buildings four years to implement measures that have a payback time of fewer than five years. Portugal requires poorly rated public buildings to make all improvements that have a payback time of fewer than eight years within three years of certification (Maldonado, Wouters, and Panek, 2008).

Opponents of the EPBD emphasize the cost of obtaining the certificates. Greeks and Bulgarians interviewed offered rough estimates of costs ranging from 1€ to 1.50€ per square meter for all buildings. The cost of obtaining an EPC for new residential buildings ranges from 150€ in the Netherlands to 410€ in Denmark (Maldonado, Wouters, and Panek, 2008). Costs escalate considerably for large buildings. The European Commission admitted that "the need to keep prices down has been especially large when apartments are rented because only small transaction costs are generally involved in these contracts and the frequency of rental can be quite high for these units" (Maldonado, Wouters, and Panek, 2008).

The directive also requires a display energy certificate (DEC) in all public buildings with more than 1,000 sq m of usable floor space. The DEC shows the building's rating and energy consumption. The definition of "public" is left up to the member countries.

Inspection of Boilers and Air Conditioning

Articles 8 and 9 of the EPBD deal with inspections of boilers and air-conditioning systems. The articles require establishment of a system to inspect hot-water boilers used for heating. States are permitted to set the inspection interval for 20- to 100-kw boilers. For boilers larger than 100 kw, inspection must be done every other year (every four years for gas boilers). The directive also mandates "one-off" inspections of the whole heating system for boilers larger than 20 kw and more than 15 years old.

The directive provides the option to forgo an inspection scheme in favor of a public education and awareness effort that offers advice to building owners about the importance of proper and regular maintenance of boilers and the benefits of ensuring proper boiler size.

Member states have been split on their choices. Finland, for example, chose a national information campaign for boiler replacement after determining that the expected savings from inspections was only 7€ per year for each system, while the expected cost of an inspection was 50€ to 100€ (Antinucci, 2008). The Dutch found evidence that periodic inspections resulted in energy savings of from 5 to 35 percent (Antinucci, 2008). Another option some countries have chosen is an inspection program for boilers larger than 100 kw and an information campaign for smaller boilers, which have smaller returns (Antinucci, 2008).

The inspection of air-conditioning systems larger than 12 kw is also mandated by Article 9. The inspection is intended to verify the operating efficiency of a system and to check that it is appropriately sized for the space it is servicing.

Experts

Each member state has the responsibility of creating a system for training and certifying the experts who will certify the buildings, provide recommendations for improving low-performing buildings, and conduct the inspection of heating and air-conditioning systems. The EPBD Concerted Action group determined that "the skills and training needs of assessors depend strongly on national procedures" (Maldonado, Wouters, and Panek, 2008). A test-based certification process is the approach taken by most states; there is greater variation in the prerequisite requirements for receiving training and taking the certification test. For example, Germany requires that an inspector of commercial buildings must be a trained architect or engineer, while Hungary requires that an inspector be a licensed surveyor (Schettler-Kohler, 2008). There are varying ideas about whether only individuals can become certified or whether an organization could become certified and then allow its employees to conduct inspections.

Calculation of Energy Performance

Article 3 of the EPBD instructs member states to establish a methodology for calculating energy performance and suggests that carbon-dioxide emissions may be used as one basis for the calculation. The actual procedures for calculating performance are left to states, but the calculations must be displayed in a "transparent manner."

The largest divide in this area is between using a modeling process to measure performance, often called an asset or design rating, and using the actual consumption of a building, often called an operational or achieved rating. In most cases, the design approach must be used for new buildings, at least initially, because new buildings lack operating data. Sweden is the exception in this respect: New Swedish buildings are certified only after construction to allow for collection of energy consumption data (Maldonado, Wouters, and Panek, 2008). States are divided on the use of asset or operational ratings for existing buildings, with those in favor of asset ratings claiming that the process is more efficient and inexpensive, while those advocating operational ratings assert that buildings often fail to perform to their designed level and thus it is more appropriate to use actual consumption.

Minimum Energy Performance Requirements

Obliging member states to set energy performance requirements is one of the most substantial achievements of the EPBD to date. All member states must develop building codes, which some did not have prior to the directive. The EPBD also requires states to review all code requirements at five-year intervals to ensure that they are up to date. The specific minimum performance requirements are still left up to the states. Generally, member states have chosen to set separate requirements for new and existing buildings and also for different types of buildings. The energy performance requirements must be applied to all new buildings as well as to renovations of buildings with more than 1,000 sq m of usable floor space.

EPBD Recast

The European Commission is currently working on a recast (revised version) of the EPBD, which is intended to strengthen the existing legislation and close loopholes. The recast proposes removing the 1,000-sq-m threshold for the minimum energy performance requirements for new construction and large renovations. It further requires member states to implement a quality-assurance program for inspectors. The requirement to disclose the energy performance certificate at sale or lease would be expanded to require disclosure in all advertisements of property for sale or lease. Finally, the recast proposes to improve the level of ambition in energy efficiency codes. This recast was proposed by the Commission in November 2008 and still has to go through several steps in order to be passed. It faces some opposition from groups of property owners who are concerned about the costs of fulfilling the requirements.

CHAPTER THREE

Australian Approaches

Australian policy for promoting energy efficiency in buildings is based on a mix of market-based, regulatory, disclosure, and financial approaches. In general, states, especially New South Wales, have pursued more aggressive energy efficiency policies than the national government has, especially market-based strategies.

Market-Based Energy Efficient Buildings Policy

Australia's history with market-based approaches to achieving energy efficient buildings is tied to its experience with carbon-dioxide-emissions trading programs. In 2003, Australia's largest state, New South Wales (whose population of 6.9 million constitutes roughly one-third of Australia's total population), started a carbon-dioxide-emissions trading program called the Greenhouse Gas Abatement Scheme (GGAS). Under GGAS, major emitters of greenhouse gases, such as power generators and industrial facilities, are required to reduce carbon emissions or purchase carbon offset credits, called New South Wales Greenhouse Gas Abatement Certificates (NGACs), to cover the difference between their carbon-dioxide-reduction target and their actual emissions.[1] In the GGAS program, building owners earn NGACs through designated "demand-side abatement" investments intended to improve the energy efficiency of buildings. The NGACs are sold to "obligated parties" to enable them to meet their carbon-dioxide-reduction targets.

In the buildings sector, NGACs are given for improvements to building assets to make them more efficient, but they are not given for operational improvements to a building's energy performance. Investments that qualify for NGACs include switching a gas-powered heating system to a more efficient electric-powered system and replacing appliances with more efficient alternatives. The amount of NGACs credited per investment is preestablished by the New South Wales government.

The experience with the GGAS buildings sector component (which formally ended on January 1, 2009) was mixed. In the first five years of the program (2003–2007), 21.5 million NGACs (31 percent of the total NGACs created) were awarded for improvements to building energy efficiency. The largest share of NGACs were earned by switching to less-carbon-intensive fuel sources for power generators. The residential sector was more active in GGAS trading than the commercial sector. The vast majority of the NGACs awarded between 2003

[1] One NGAC is equal to one ton of carbon dioxide abated.

and 2007 for demand-side abatement activities (18 million, or 84 percent) were earned in the residential sector, and a relatively modest 1.1 million were earned in the commercial sector.

Several factors led to a low uptake of GGAS incentives in the commercial sector and explained the relative success in the residential sector. Most important was the business model adopted by NGAC-earning firms. In the residential sector, most demand-side abatement NGACs were earned by a small number of firms that bought large quantities of CFLs and low-flow shower heads and distributed them to homeowners free of charge or at a large discount. These firms earned a profit based on the margin between the market price of the NGACs and the cost of the appliances. The business model of purchasing small, energy efficient appliances in bulk and distributing them to building owners was more successful in the residential sector than in the commercial sector because such appliances are used more in homes than in commercial buildings (Crossley, 2008).

Another reason for the low uptake of demand-side abatement NGACs in the commercial sector was their relatively low value. Electricity in Australia is inexpensive (about 3 to 4 cents per kWh) and represents a small fraction of the cost of doing business. Given the low cost of electricity and the low market prices of NGACs, the process for earning an NGAC rarely warranted the effort (Lend Lease Corporation, Lincolne Scott, and Advanced Environmental, 2009).

Despite the modest success of the demand-side abatement component in the residential sector, it has been criticized for several reasons. First, the program allowed firms to earn credits based on the distribution of energy efficient appliances, rather than actual reductions in energy use. Indeed, an independent market study found that only about half of the CFLs and efficient shower heads distributed to homeowners were actually installed.

The second, more fundamental criticism was that the GGAS system is focused primarily on achieving carbon-dioxide abatement from the electricity and industrial sectors—the most costly segments of the economy—and only indirectly addresses energy efficient buildings, potentially one of the most economical means of achieving large-scale carbon-dioxide reduction.[2] The theory implicit in a carbon-dioxide-emissions scheme is that placing a price on carbon-dioxide emissions will increase energy costs, creating incentives for building owners to implement improvements that reduce energy consumption. However, the increased cost of electricity does not necessarily translate into reduced consumption, for several reasons. First, the increased cost is small relative to the overall cost of doing business and may be insufficient to change energy use. Second, building owners and tenants do not always have sufficient information or time to consider cost-effective energy efficiency investments. Third, as noted above, owners and tenants may have split incentives in commercial buildings. Because of these barriers, critics of the GGAS system argue that an efficient buildings program would be one that squarely puts the obligation to reduce emissions of carbon dioxide on utilities and building owners.[3]

In response to this criticism and the mixed success of the GGAS program in the commercial sector, several Australian states have recently begun a second generation of market-based energy efficiency programs. In these second-generation programs, white certificates are purchased by utilities to meet energy-consumption-reduction targets, rather than by power

[2] Interview with Australian building developer, April 8, 2009.

[3] Interview with Australian building developer, April 2, 2009.

generators and industry to meet carbon-dioxide-emission-reduction targets. For example, in the New South Wales Energy Efficiency Trading Scheme (NEET), now called the Energy Efficiency Trading Scheme (ETS), energy retailers are required to meet electricity-reduction targets. These targets can be met by implementing demand-side abatement activities or by purchasing white certificates awarded to building owners who improve the efficiency assets of a building or improve the building's overall measured energy efficiency performance, as measured by a National Australian Built Environment Rating System (NABERS) score. Because the program was created on January 1, 2009, little data are available yet to assess its effectiveness.

Victoria has a similar market-based program, called the Victorian Energy Efficiency Target Scheme (VEET). VEET is similar to the New South Wales program in that energy retailers are required to meet electricity-consumption-reduction targets either by implementing demand-side abatement programs or by purchasing white certificates. However, in VEET, white certificates can be earned only by residential building owners. In addition, VEET program participants earn white certificates through improvements to the assets of buildings, not on the basis of an improved energy performance score. VEET was also implemented in January 2009, and it is too early to assess its success.

The Australian states' new programs were created in the context of a forthcoming national carbon-dioxide-emissions trading program, called the Carbon Pollution Reduction Scheme, which the Australian government intends to put in place in 2010. Similar to the European and New South Wales carbon-dioxide-emissions trading schemes, the new program is to be based on a cap-and-trade system for carbon-dioxide emissions in Australia. However, the effect the program will have on buildings is uncertain.

Several options are possible. The national program could ignore the buildings sector and allow state-run efficiency trading programs to work to (independently) complement it. Alternatively, the national government could create a system similar to the GGAS program, in which building owners would be able to earn and sell carbon-dioxide credits for energy efficiency improvements made to buildings. This system is appealing, because it would create a single, cohesive market for carbon-dioxide credits. However, as in the GGAS system, market barriers such as imperfect information, high transaction costs, and split incentives might prevent the program from fully realizing the energy efficiency potential available in commercial real estate. A third option would be to have the government more aggressively pursue energy efficiency by creating a national efficiency trading scheme, similar to NEET, in which energy retailers would be obligated to reduce electricity consumption or purchase white certificates to meet their targets.

A fourth alternative, championed by Australian multinational building and property developer Lend Lease Corporation, is a scheme in which commercial-building owners themselves (rather than electricity retailers) would be required to meet energy-reduction targets. In this proposed program, the government would set long-term electricity-reduction targets for commercial real estate. Buildings that consume less energy per leasable square foot would earn white certificates; buildings that consume more energy would be required to either reduce their electricity usage or purchase white certificates from the owners of more efficient buildings. Unlike the NEET program, in which building owners voluntarily participated, the proposed scheme would be mandatory for all commercial buildings. Building owners would be subject to both the carrot of earning white certificates and the stick of penalties if their buildings are less efficient than the industry average.

Building Codes and Performance Ratings

Australia uses building codes and energy performance rating systems in addition to market-based approaches to promote building energy efficiency.

Building codes in Australia are regulated at the national level. In the 2006 revision of the Building Code of Australia (BCA), new residential, commercial, and public sector buildings and major retrofits (i.e., those whose cost equals more than one-half the assessed value of the building) are subject to meeting the code. The code prescribes standards for nearly all components of buildings, including heating and ventilation systems, insulation, and plumbing, to ensure that new buildings are acceptably energy efficient.

To complement the BCA—a prescriptive program designed to ensure that minimum energy efficiency standards are met—several states have adopted their own regulations to strengthen efficiency standards for new and retrofitted buildings. In New South Wales, every development application for residential buildings is required to have a Buildings Sustainability Index (BASIX) certificate. BASIX is a software tool that calculates the potential energy performance of a building, based on a wide range of design components. Unlike the BCA, BASIX is flexible, in that it provides many ways in which a building owner can configure a building to achieve a satisfactory rating. In Victoria, new residential buildings are required to be certified with a five-star rating, as assessed by the Australian Green Building Council's Green Star program. The Green Star program is a design-based energy performance rating analogous to the U.S. Green Building Council's LEED system; a five-star Green Star rating is equivalent to a LEED gold standard.[4] Like BASIX—and unlike the BCA—Green Star is a flexible, outcome-based program in which building owners can achieve required ratings in a variety of ways. Western Australia and Queensland also require new residential buildings to achieve a five-star rating.

BASIX and Green Star are design-based systems, but Australia also uses the NABERS operational-based energy performance rating system, which applies primarily to existing buildings. In Queensland, all existing commercial buildings are required to achieve a four-star NABERS rating by 2010. In all other states, NABERS remains a voluntary program.

State governments have used energy performance ratings for public buildings in "lead-by-example" approaches to encourage demand for energy efficient commercial-building space. For example, the Queensland state government leases office space only in buildings that have at least a four-star Green Star rating (equivalent to a LEED silver standard). Other state government agencies and authorities require four-star or higher Green Star ratings in publicly owned or leased buildings as well. The Australian Department of Defence also uses Green Star rating tools in the design and construction of its buildings. But by and large, state and local governments have been more aggressive than the national government in requiring energy performance ratings in publicly owned or leased buildings.

Disclosure and Energy Audits

The Council of Australian Governments (COAG)—an organization comprising the Prime Minister and all the state governors—is planning to put a European-style energy performance

[4] Interview with Australian non-governmental organization (NGO) director, April 7, 2009.

disclosure system into effect in 2010. This program is still in the design phase, and the sectors to which it will apply and the type of energy performance rating standard it will use (e.g., Green Star or NABERS) are unclear.

The national government also requires all large energy-consuming businesses (those that consume more than 0.5 petajoules, or 139 GWh, per year) to perform Energy Efficiency Opportunities reports every four years. These reports include an assessment of the energy consumption practices of the business and cost-benefit analyses of energy efficiency investments. This requirement currently applies to roughly 210 businesses. Whether energy efficiency investments that have a four-year payback period or less should be mandated is currently being debated. In New South Wales, large energy-consuming businesses (those that consume more than 10 GWh per year) must perform energy audits and cost-benefit analyses for potential investments. All Energy Savings Action Plans must be updated every four years. Unlike the Energy Efficiency Opportunities program, investments can be either operational (process-related) or structural (changes to the assets of a building). Reports on all investments with a payback period of four years or less are mandated.

Grant and Rebate Programs

Australia has budgeted limited amounts of public funds for grant and rebate programs to improve energy efficiency of buildings. In 2008, the national government allocated AU $90 million (U.S. $64 million) for competitive grants for energy efficiency improvements to buildings. The national government also allocates money for energy efficiency R&D projects. Similarly, New South Wales, Victoria, and Queensland all have funds allocated for energy efficiency R&D projects.

One innovative proposal championed by the Australian Sustainable Built Environment Council is "green depreciation." A green-depreciation program would allow owners of commercial buildings accelerated depreciation for buildings or building assets that meet specified energy performance standards. Accelerated depreciation effectively allows businesses to defer corporate income taxes to future years. While a green-depreciation program is fiscally neutral in nominal terms, the ability to defer tax payments represents a net present value subsidy to commercial building owners, because of the time value of money. Advocates of green depreciation argue that the program spreads the costs of energy efficiency investments. When a capital investment is made to improve the efficiency of a building, tax payments are low; as the economic returns for those efficiency improvements are realized, tax payments increase. This helps stabilize the balance sheets of businesses investing in energy efficiency.

The Decentralized Approach

Australia has a diverse portfolio of programs at the national and state levels that use information, regulation, and financial incentives to promote energy efficient buildings. Historically, Australia's approach to energy efficient buildings was motivated primarily by climate-change concerns. Australia's signature efficient building programs—the market-based white-certificate programs—are rooted in the country's relatively long history with carbon-dioxide emissions programs. However, concern about the unrealized potential for economically beneficial energy efficiency gains has led Australia to adopt a more targeted approach. The second generation of white-certificate programs—NEET and VEET—along with the deployment of stricter building codes, mandatory energy audits, and energy performance rating systems, represents an attempt to deal with energy efficiency as an economically desirable end in itself, not just as a means to reduce carbon-dioxide emissions. These policies also reflect the belief that price signals alone are insufficient to induce significant improvements in energy efficiency. A diverse portfolio of policies that address limited information, bounded rationality, and the split-incentive problem inherent in tenant-occupied buildings is assumed to be needed to create the appropriate incentives for energy efficiency investments.

Differing policy motivations can also help explain why the state governments have generally been more aggressive than the national government in implementing energy efficient buildings policies. In Australia, state-owned utilities are responsible for building power-generation plants. Several analysts close to developments in Australia have claimed that the states' fiscal obligation to meet electricity demand with sufficient supply has been a primary driver of aggressive energy efficiency policies at the state level.[5] Because reducing energy demand is cheaper than building additional electricity-generation capacity, cash-strapped states have had a powerful fiscal incentive to encourage energy efficiency.

Australia's portfolio of policies reflects the diversity of the commercial real-estate sector. For new buildings, regulatory policies such as building codes and design-based energy performance ratings are perhaps most appropriate. However, policies focused exclusively on new buildings are insufficient given the very low turnover rate in commercial buildings. White-certificate programs and mandatory energy audit programs are more appropriate for the existing building stock.

---

[5] Interview with Australian state government official, April 6, 2009.

CHAPTER FOUR

Key Issues in Buildings Energy Efficiency Programs

As we have seen, the EU and Australia have instituted significant new public policies to promote energy efficiency in the "built environment." Many of these public policies were motivated by the same concerns that led to the pioneering voluntary initiatives of Green Building Councils (especially the LEED design certification program) and the EPA's ENERGY STAR system for buildings.

However, policy initiatives on both continents are relatively new, have been recently modified, and are yet to be finalized. Further, in both Europe and Australia, there is wide variety in the transposition of the general approach at the national-government level (in the EU) or in state-level initiatives (in Australia). There has been little objective, peer-reviewed research to date on the effects of various approaches on energy efficiency.

Despite the diversity of detail, energy efficiency policy initiatives in Europe and Australia have been assembled from common building blocks:

- Building codes
- Energy design or use certificates
- Special minimum rating requirements or display obligations for public buildings
- Benchmarks or grading systems
- Qualified inspectors, including quality-assurance programs and standardized energy modeling software
- Incentives (including certificate trading systems).

Building Codes

Discussion

Building codes are effective in bringing about energy efficiency gains. They define standards that must be met in new building construction or major renovation, they are enforced consistently within jurisdictions, and they can set very specific minimum thermal efficiency standards for building envelopes; for heating, ventilating, and air-conditioning (HVAC); for boiler systems; or for other variables that make a difference in the energy efficiency of buildings.

Tightened building codes are generally considered responsible for significant improvements in the energy performance of buildings throughout the developed world between 1980 and 2000. For example, until Greece adopted a national building code based on Germany's code, it had no requirement for thermal insulation in the outer walls of buildings.[1] In the UK, energy efficiency regulations, grant schemes, and equipment labeling and standards implemented in the mid-1970s and thereafter reduced total energy use in housing by approximately 14 percent. Building codes adopted in 1965 and updated five times since then were responsible for half of the aggregate energy savings (Shorrock, 2001).

The 2002 version of the EPBD specified that all EU member states must have building codes with energy efficiency elements, although it left to the states' discretion the actual performance or design values. This provision was intended to require adoption of building codes by several former Soviet bloc countries that were then negotiating accession agreements to join the EU but did not have any national building codes.[2] (Ten new member states acceded to the EU in 2004, and Bulgaria and Romania joined in 2006.)

The main drawback of stricter building codes as a strategy to improve energy efficiency is that they take time to significantly affect overall energy use in the sector. In normal years, only about 3 percent of the building stock of a developed country is built or renovated. (In the present global economic slowdown, building-start rates are well below even that.) The European Commission estimates that buildings undergo major renovation once every 25 to 40 years on average (European Commission, 2008). On the other hand, step changes in code requirements are a gift that keeps on giving, in that energy efficiency requirements mandated at initial construction (for insulation, windows, and major heating and cooling systems) reliably save energy for the lifetime of the building.

As an economic matter, however, building codes that significantly raise the cost of construction or renovation tend to inhibit new construction on the margin and are resisted by industry segments that specialize in new construction and lower-cost buildings, in particular. But energy efficiency–related requirements that add negligible costs in initial construction (basic thermal insulation of exterior walls and ceilings, for example) have a very high economic payoff.

The main issues associated with developing building codes are the frequency with which they are updated in light of new technology, whether they can be effectively implemented by inspectors, and whether they encourage or inhibit innovation.

In Europe, building codes are set at the national or subnational level. The EPBD specifies that member states must review their codes every five years, although there is no affirmative obligation to update them. There are wide variations in code requirements, partly because of the range of climatic conditions and building types within the EU. And in Australia, the national building code program, the BCA, recognizes six distinct climatic zones.[3]

The consistency of compliance with code requirements is sometimes a problem, especially in poorer countries. One study found that in developing countries, 70 percent of new buildings complied with the codes on paper, but only 30 percent did so in reality (Deringer, 2004). A Bulgarian expert reported that compliance with building codes, which are still very new in the country, is very low, and inspector corruption is widespread.[4] To deal with this problem, Bul-

[1] Interview with Greek developer, April 10, 2009.

[2] Interview with European Commission official, January 28, 2009; interview with Bulgarian NGO official, March 23, 2009.

[3] Interview with Australian state government official, April 6, 2009.

[4] Interview with Bulgarian NGO official, March 23, 2009.

garia has set up a centralized Energy Efficiency Agency, which has the power to stop construction of buildings that do not meet requirements and is the sole issuer of compliance certificates that allow sale, transfer, or rehabilitation of structures.[5]

There is also a choice between prescriptive and performance targets for building-code energy requirements. Prescriptive approaches specify minimum materials characteristics (insulation values, window-glass energy ratings), while performance approaches mandate minimum energy efficiency characteristics and allow the architect or builder to determine how to achieve them. The prescriptive approach saves on calculation costs, since building inspectors do not need sophisticated training, nor do they make as many calculations to assess compliance as are necessary under a performance approach. The performance approach allows for more interesting innovations in energy savings on the part of building designers, but it requires more highly trained building officials and inspectors.[6] One experienced European energy consultant suggested that prescriptive approaches can be more reliable and can encourage the market to develop products that meet the requirements. He added that performance calculations usually reward complicated solutions, while practical experience shows that it is better to keep things simple and do them well.[7]

Observations

Adding energy efficiency requirements to building codes is a fundamental starting point for improving the energy efficiency of a nation's building stock. Nationwide consistency of energy-related aspects of codes can help building-materials manufacturers standardize products and can simplify code implementation and enforcement. However, countries with a wide range of climatic conditions may achieve more cost-effective outcomes by customizing building codes to regional climatic characteristics. Performance-based energy provisions of building codes are superior in principle, as they encourage innovative outcomes-based design approaches. They are difficult to implement, however, as they require more highly trained building inspectors and more sophisticated instrumentation. Performance-based codes make the most sense in jurisdictions where they mirror performance certificate programs, especially if the measured criteria are the same for all programs.

Certificates

Discussion

The intent of all certificate programs is to encourage more energy efficient choices in building design (including siting), building management, and (when carbon-dioxide emissions are included in certification decisions) choice of fuels for heating and cooling. Certificate programs inform choices by providing information to building owners, lessees, and purchasers about the design characteristics or actual energy performance of buildings they may be considering buying, leasing, or renovating. Certificate programs not only seek to redress the problem

---

[5] Interview with Bulgarian NGO official, March 31, 2009. Bulgarian energy efficiency programs have been supported since the late 1990s by United States Agency for International Development programs funded under the Support to Eastern European Democracies Act.

[6] Interview with Portuguese academic, March 25, 2009; see also United Nations Environment Program, 2007, p. 17.

[7] Email exchange with British energy consultant, June 27, 2009.

of inadequate information, they also help market participants understand what the compiled information on energy design or use means in a broader context. The latter is the role of ratings, or benchmarks. The EU allows member states to decide whether the EPC required by the EPBD for building transactions involving more than 1,000 sq m of space is based on design or operational criteria.

The first design rating scheme in Europe was the UK's Building Research Establishment Environmental Assessment Method (BREEAM), which was launched in 1990. It was a voluntary program used primarily in the office sector, but many government projects now require a minimum BREEAM rating.[8] More than half of the property investors surveyed in 2008 and 2007 reported that they consider BREEAM ratings "important" for investment decisions (GVA Grimley, 2008).

In the United States, a voluntary asset (design) rating system (the LEED system) was developed by the U.S. Green Building Council, and a voluntary operational ratings system was created by extension of the EPA's and Department of Energy's ENERGY STAR appliance rating program to office and residential buildings. Both are based on comparative benchmarks (LEED's platinum, gold, and silver certifications and ENERGY STAR ratings).

Europe and Australia now make wide use of both asset and operational ratings and, in various combinations, have made them mandatory for certain transactions.[9] As with building codes, however, each country (and in some cases, each subnational jurisdiction) has selected its own benchmarking levels for ratings.

Both asset and operational ratings have advantages and disadvantages. An asset rating with benchmarks by building type facilitates building-to-building comparisons within the scope of a particular national or subnational scheme. An asset rating also emphasizes the energy efficiency *potential* of the building being rated. The best asset rating programs encourage design innovation to reach the highest energy rating at the lowest cost. Asset ratings based on design also sidestep the split-incentive problem in multitenant buildings, where building owners do not reap the economic benefits of energy cost savings when energy costs are paid by tenants. With a good asset rating, the owner should be able to recoup efficiency investments through higher rentals.[10]

The main disadvantages of asset ratings are that they can give a false impression of a building's actual energy performance and discourage making improvements in older buildings. It is well documented that most buildings' actual energy consumption tends to be considerably more than the consumption projected by the design rating, which is based on ideal management techniques. In some cases, the discrepancy is accounted for by tenant behavior or changes in use (e.g., addition of a data center in an office building). In other cases, the builder may not have completely followed the design. Another disadvantage of reliance on design ratings is that many older buildings cannot ever hope to qualify for top rankings, because of basic design characteristics. Under asset design ratings, owners of older buildings may be dis-

---

[8] Email exchange with UK energy consultant, June 27, 2009.

[9] As noted earlier, CEN, the EU's standards body, developed definitions for asset and operational ratings in European Standard EN 15603. The Australian rating scheme is NABERS.

[10] One expert we interviewed suggested that only in those office sectors that are highly sensitive to reputation are higher ratings reliably translated into higher rents. In the retail sector, all that matters are "location and footfall" (interview with British trade association official, March 24, 2009). As noted below, the only econometric studies of the value of ratings thus far have been conducted in the office and residential real-estate markets.

couraged from renovation or making management changes.[11] (For example, it may be feasible to renovate a building only from a D rating to a C rating, which would result in little or no market advantage, but the actual energy saved by such an investment might be more than that saved by constructing an A-rated building rather than a B-rated building.)

An operational-based certificate that assembles data on actual energy supplies used by a particular building and displays the information in a standard format has the advantage that it is based on hard data with an audit trail. For existing buildings, operational certificates also obviate the need to look behind walls or above ceilings. What counts in most such systems is the energy actually consumed and how drafty the building is. Another advantage of operational certificates is that they can include practical recommendations for improvements in energy performance.[12] Building owners thus get consulting advice along with the energy performance information. As noted above, some countries, including Portugal and Denmark, have even required building owners to implement some of the performance certificate recommendations.[13]

A disadvantage of operationally based certificates is that they are not available for new construction and they are hard to compile for multitenant buildings whose owners do not have access to tenant energy-consumption data. Especially in the case of residential buildings, privacy issues can also be raised. (Article 7.1 of the EPBD recognizes this difficulty, explicitly allowing the use of assessments of "representative apartments" or the "entire building" in multi-unit complexes.) In the UK, a Landlord's Energy Statement–Tenant's Energy Review system has been developed to address this problem (British Property Federation, n.d.).

Useful benchmarking with operationally based certificates also requires standardizing for various uses of buildings of the same type (based on hours of occupation, data center equipment, entertainment complexes of various types, etc.). If the base period is too short, measured energy use will be affected by the vagaries of weather,[14] but performance data covering too long a base period can act as a disincentive to efficiency-directed renovation, since a building continues to carry pre-renovation energy consumption data well into the future, affecting its rating (Lend Lease Corporation, Lincolne Scott, and Advanced Environmental, 2009).

Operationally based ratings really measure occupant behavior, not building capability. For this reason, European Commission officials prefer design ratings, pointing out that the relative impact of occupant behavior increases with increases in building shell performance, citing an example of 42 identical houses built in Germany with identical passive-energy design features. Actual energy use in those structures is said to vary by a factor of seven.[15]

---

[11] Interview with British trade association official, March 24, 2009.

[12] An energy consultant cited the example of the recent review of a government building given a G (lowest) operational rating. Consultants found a faulty electricity meter, and although the building was still rated G, the government received a substantial refund from the utility. With better management of the building, an F grade was achieved. With better controls, perhaps an E can be achieved. A C is possible with capital investment having a 7- to 10-year payback (email from UK energy consultant, June 27, 2009).

[13] The inclusion of operational recommendations in performance certificates was first implemented in the Danish national program (Kjaerbye, 2008). In the recast of the EPBD, a requirement to implement cost-effective recommendations was considered, but it was rejected as imposing a mandate on member states that was not justified by subsidiarity.

[14] In the UK, data are amalgamated over a three-year period to average out weather effects (interview with British NGO employee).

[15] Interview with European Commission official, April 16, 2009.

A common issue associated with both design and performance certificate systems is that of presenting the data and rankings objectively to owners, lessees, and prospective buyers in a way that is understandable and that provides incentives to use energy efficiently. Each jurisdiction has struggled with this challenge. One European building owners' representative charged that certificates were designed for the "defamation of older buildings."[16] Most European countries have designed their building certificates to resemble the well-understood and popular European appliance energy efficiency ratings, with rankings from A to G. EU countries have approached the problem of choosing threshold levels for A-to-G ratings by setting percentages above or below the average energy use of a reference building of similar type and size. In Germany, the certificates show design and performance ratings side by side. In the UK, a box in the upper right-hand corner of the certificate shows estimated emissions of carbon dioxide, based on a combination of energy use and fuel type.[17]

In the European system, the benchmark values for letter ratings are set nationally rather than across the entire EU. The requirements can vary widely between countries (e.g., for building skin thermal efficiency, window performance, and energy use per square meter). A European Commission official acknowledged the inconsistencies among national ratings, noting that some of the inconsistencies were appropriate variations due to climatic conditions, but stated that the fundamental reason was the member states' view that these details were matters for national implementation under the principle of subsidiarity. The Commission view is that except in the case of international companies and hotel chains that may wish to set consistent worldwide energy-use policies (for which the voluntary LEED rating system is available), real-estate transactions generally involve comparisons between buildings in one national jurisdiction, and thus the inconsistencies have no practical impact on efficiency choices.[18]

Observations

Certificate programs based on building inspections are the cornerstone of both the European EPBD and Australian buildings energy efficiency programs. The central public policy choice is whether to base consumer information on asset ratings or measured energy use, or, as is done in some countries, both. Asset ratings measure a building's capabilities, rather than the behavior (good or bad) of recent occupants. Asset ratings also are the only basis upon which unbuilt designs or as-yet-unoccupied buildings can be judged, and they reflect decisions the building owner can control. In contrast, performance ratings focus on the public policy goal of improved efficiency in energy use. Performance ratings are audited more easily and can be tracked by third parties (such as utilities), although if the base period is too short, they can be distorted by variations in the weather. Some form of performance rating could contribute to efforts to solve the split-incentive problem if it underpinned "green leases."[19] The EPBD requires certificates to be provided when buildings are constructed, sold, or rented. But purchase settlements may not be the best occasion on which to communicate energy performance characteristics, since at that point, the sales price is typically agreed on and many other docu-

---

[16] Interview with European building owner association official, April 10, 2009.

[17] Interview with British NGO official, March 19, 2009.

[18] Interview with European Commission official, April 16, 2009.

[19] Green leases provide tenants a rental discount if they meet specified energy consumption targets (interview with Australian building developer, April 2, 2009).

ments and disclosures are being exchanged. That is a main reason for the proposal in the EU's EPBD recast to require EPC disclosure in property listings and advertisements. In light of the growing importance of energy use in establishing building value, EPCs may also be useful during mortgage transactions, including refinancings.

Promoting Energy Efficiency in Public Buildings

Discussion

In both the EU and Australia, public policy programs to promote energy efficiency in buildings place public buildings in a special category. Public buildings, especially those owned by national, state, or local governments, are sometimes considered showcases for new technologies. They present an opportunity to demonstrate the influence of energy consumption disclosure on efficiency behavior.

In Australia, the state and federal governments are estimated to use 40 percent of the leased office space. For a number of years, both Victoria and New South Wales and at least one commonwealth ministry have had an announced policy of leasing only office space that qualifies for at least a four-star Green Star energy performance rating (approximately equal to a LEED silver rating).[20] This has driven developers to certify all new space at this level to avoid foreclosing the possibility that the space might be leased for government use at some time in the future.[21] Nevertheless, there is as yet no national requirement to post Green Star or NABERS ratings in public buildings or to make them systematically available.

In the EU, DECs are required to be posted in public buildings that have more than 1,000 sq m of floor space as part of the implementation of the EPBD. The DEC program is based on similar national programs pioneered in Germany and Denmark. Each member state may form its own definition of the "public" buildings to which it applies (the EPBD specifies only "public authorities" and "institutions providing public services to a large number of persons and thereby visited frequently by these persons").[22] The EPBD also requires that certificates be "not older than" 10 years and that they be placed in "a prominent place clearly visible to the public." A number of questions about the DEC program have arisen: Does the DEC requirement apply to publicly regulated utilities? Does it apply to airports and train stations? Does being posted in a "place clearly visible to the public" require posting on the Internet? Different countries have approached these questions in local law and administrative guidance in different ways.

The intent of DECs is similar to that of voluntary schemes in the United States: to raise public awareness of buildings' energy consumption, with the public sector in the vanguard, and to provide an incentive for public entities to improve the efficiency of existing buildings and the design of those to come.

Unfortunately, many large public buildings have functions that by their nature require greater energy intensity, although significant energy efficiency gains can still be made. In many countries, public buildings tend to be older and to have large open spaces and high visitor

[20] Interview with Australian NGO official, April 7, 2009.

[21] Interview with state government energy efficiency official, Victoria, April 6, 2009.

[22] Portugal has the most expansive definition, covering any building generally open to the public, including shopping centers, sports stadiums, and hospitals.

counts. Many contain specialized service functions, including data centers. The challenge, as noted earlier, is to find appropriate benchmarks to evaluate realized efficiencies. Additionally, public sector budgets, especially at provincial and local levels, have been reduced in many countries, making it difficult to find funding for even highly cost-effective renovations. Political leaders (especially at the local level) in several European countries have been loath to draw attention to the energy shortcomings of their stock of public buildings.[23]

Faced with such difficulties, the European Commission has tried to support municipalities that adhere to the "Covenant of Mayors," making a commitment to reduce emissions of carbon dioxide in their cities by more than the EU's 20 percent goal for 2020.[24] Policies to improve the energy efficiency of buildings are among the efforts of this group of generally larger municipalities.

In many countries, public sector entities lease space in buildings that also have other commercial uses. Does that mean that a DEC should be prepared for the entire building or only for that portion occupied by the government office? As we have noted, the Australian national government and the state governments of Victoria and New South Wales will lease only four-star-rated space, which has had the effect of providing incentives to the broader new-built and renovated commercial office-space market. In the UK, responsibility for implementing the EPBD is vested in the Department of Communities and Local Government, which has set as its first priority the calculation and display of DECs for buildings with more than 1,000 sq m of floor space that are wholly occupied by national government agencies. Sorting out what obligations the government has when it occupies a large building it shares with others will be left to a later date.[25]

Observations

In principle, public buildings should be subject to at least the same energy efficiency rules applied to comparable private sector buildings in any jurisdiction. Both the EU and Australia follow this principle but go beyond it in two important respects. The Australian approach is to set a minimum Green Star (asset rating) efficiency level for privately owned buildings the government would consider leasing. The public sector's market power is so significant that this policy drives the behavior of the developers supplying the commercial lease market. In Europe, the additional obligation on the public sector is the requirement of disclosure in DECs. In many cases, the public sector is the owner as well as the occupant of a building (although many governments own properties through one ministry or entity and have other agencies serving as tenants); in other cases, public sector agencies or institutions offering public services use space leased from private owners. Because the public sector generally has control over its buildings (eliminating the split-incentive and privacy issues noted above), it would seem to be preferable for display certificates to be based on actual energy usage rather than design criteria, if they do not include both indicators. Operational certificates are also inexpensive to prepare, which should help strapped public sector budgets.

---

[23] Interview with European Commission official, April 16, 2009.

[24] Ibid.

[25] Interview with British NGO official, March 19, 2009. As noted earlier, the Landlord's Energy Statement methodology is an option for DEC presentation of data on energy use in multitenant buildings.

Training and Certification of Experts

Discussion

EU countries, despite years of discussion (even prior to the adoption of the landmark EPBD in 2002), found it so difficult to train and certify sufficient numbers of experts to be able to provide EPCs for sale or lease transactions that they deferred the EPBD's implementation date by three years. Even so, only six countries were ready to implement it in January 2009;[26] at least three countries—Germany, Denmark, and Ireland—merely continued existing national programs.

Several issues have caused complications in programs to develop and certify experts. After protracted negotiations in the UK, for example, the government ended up recognizing a number of certification authorities and protocols. This obviated the risk that one accreditation body and its recognized inspectors would have inordinate market power in the issuance and collection of fees from certificates, but it introduced into the market what one observer called "bottom feeders," who offered "stack 'em high, sell 'em cheap" EPCs based on standardized language.[27] Such certificates lack the value of recommendations tailored to specific buildings. In other countries, engineering or technical groups have sought exclusivity in certificate issuance and have even proposed minimum fees for services.[28]

Another issue has been the need for the greatest numbers of expert inspectors at the outset of a certificate program. It is estimated, for example, that there are 1.5 million commercial buildings in the UK, and perhaps 10 percent are involved in leases or sale in any given year. This implies a first-year requirement (EPCs are valid for 10 years) of 150,000 EPCs for Britain's commercial sector alone. The UK presently has 1,200 experts certified by one accreditation authority and perhaps only 2,000 to 2,500 accredited in all of Britain (not including Scotland or Northern Ireland).[29] This implies a heavy initial workload and a lack of experience that could affect the credibility of the initial certificates. As of April 2009, Bruxelles-Capitale, the Belgian regional host of the European Commission's headquarters facilities, still did not have a functioning inspection/certificate program, because it lacked certified experts.[30]

In its review of member state compliance, the European Commission noted that many member states do not have a functioning quality-assurance program. Accrediting bodies do not randomly audit certificates, and there is no continuing-education program for experts who have been certified. Some member states do not require experts to visit buildings at all; certificates are issued on the basis of energy-use data submitted by the building owner. Denmark, one of the first European countries to implement an EPC scheme (in 1997), ran into credibility problems with its certificates, and those problems affected usage patterns. Denmark revised its system in 2006 to specify data quality.[31] Based on "numerous complaints" about certificates

---

[26] Interview with Portuguese academic, March 25, 2009.

[27] Interview with British trade association official, March 24, 2009.

[28] Interview with Greek developer, March 23, 2009; interview with Greek academic, March 23, 2009.

[29] Interview with British NGO official, March 24, 2009.

[30] Interview with European Commission official, April 16, 2009; interview with construction equipment executive, March 31, 2009.

[31] In the Danish system, data acquired from meter reading allows a rating of 1, while "computation by experts based on building envelope inspection" allows a rating of 6 (Jensen and Hansen, 2007).

issued on the basis of poor evaluations and statements given in public consultations, the European Commission included a provision in the EPBD recast requiring all member states to have a formal quality-assurance program for inspections and certificates (European Commission, 2008, p. 45).

A further issue concerns whether competent authorities require the experts to be independent of building owners or other interested parties. For example, can architectural firms, engineering firms, or developers have accredited certificate-issuing experts on staff to issue EPCs for buildings in which the employer has a financial interest? About half of the EU member states allow such related parties to issue EPCs.[32] The directive requires only that member states ensure that the certification and inspections be "carried out in an independent manner by qualified experts whether operating as sole traders or employed by public or private enterprise bodies" (Article 10). Commission officials admit that this is a "delicate issue" and that it would not be fully resolved by the recast, which directs member states to have inspections carried out by "accredited experts, whose independence is to be guaranteed on the basis of objective criteria" (European Commission, 2008, Article 16).[33]

Even if experts are fully independent of building owners or other interested parties, EPCs that provide energy design ratings on large commercial buildings will add to the value of such buildings, as is seen currently with top LEED rankings. In some countries, consideration may need to be given to a compensation model for inspectors to guard against the pressures of financial conflicts of interest, perhaps by requiring the selection of the examining expert to be made objectively by the accrediting body or rotated regularly.

When 10-year EPCs are based on asset (design) ratings, another issue arises, namely whether the as-built or as-renovated structure complies with the energy efficiency–related requirements of the design. For example, is the insulation level equal to that specified by the designer? Are the windows equal to or better than specifications? Fortunately, most developed-country jurisdictions have well-established procedures for inspection by public or independent private consultant engineers to assure that buildings are built as specified. Such inspections address safety concerns and protect the interests of insurers and mortgage holders. Owners also commission third-party assessors to verify builders' work for contractual reasons. This system of sign-offs can be adapted to check that as-built structures comply with energy efficiency stipulations in EPCs as well (i.e., those beyond building-code energy efficiency minima for high-rated buildings). Some high-end international developers do this now on their own account, but it is an issue to consider when adopting a public policy approach based on asset ratings.[34]

Observations

Successful programs for energy efficiency in buildings depend on the quality and impartiality of experts who review the designs and inspect the finished buildings. If these experts are credible, not only do such certificates add considerable market value to buildings (or decrease value), they also assist programs aimed at changing consumer behavior. Buildings energy efficiency programs are thus only as good as the experts charged with implementing them. The challenge is to specify training and inspection protocols—and quality-assurance programs—that

---

[32] Interview with Portuguese academic, March 25, 2009.

[33] Also, interview with European Commission official, April 16, 2009.

[34] Interview with executive of Australian development company, April 16, 2009.

guarantee credibility without imposing unnecessary administrative burden and cost. Costs can be reduced by standardization of testing protocols, software, and certification training, along with the involvement of utilities in supplying normalized data. It would also be reasonable to involve experts in a feedback loop: Allowing experts who assess building performance to give feedback to designers and owners could result in more cost-effective strategies.

White-Certificate Programs

Discussion

A white certificate has come to mean a tradable "right" that is accorded to an energy user who has achieved energy efficiency gains, or "abatements." The first formalized white-certificate program was New South Wales' 2004 GGAS mechanism. White-certificate programs were subsequently established in Italy (2006) and France (2007). In each such system, the parties earning white certificates can sell them to "obligated parties," typically utilities or large industrial users that have energy or carbon-dioxide reduction requirements. White-certificate programs thus are not *building* energy efficiency programs per se, but because many of the economically viable, verifiable savings are in commercial real estate, white certificates can be a driver of energy efficiency investments in this sector.

The main challenge for white-certificate programs is limiting the award of certificates to users that make improvements beyond those of a baseline, business-as-usual case and avoiding free-riders or wasting resources on subsidies of investments that would have occurred anyway. A related challenge is avoiding the rewarding of behavior that is mandatory for a class of users or otherwise merely compliant with law. For example, in Australia, many of the white certificates awarded under the GGAS system went to consolidators who provided free or heavily discounted CFLs or efficient shower heads to residential users. If some of these investments had been made voluntarily or had been required under building codes for new construction or renovation, the white certificates would have been redundant. Verification is also an issue: In Australia, retrospective studies have shown that about half of the CFLs and shower heads provided by consolidators in the early days of GGAS were not actually installed.

In Italy, where utilities and large industrial users are the obligated parties in a white-certificate system, eligibility is determined by specific categories of investments and preestablished definitions of energy-saving investments. Residential users purchasing appliances rated A or better qualify for white certificates, as do building owners who install four-star or better boilers and biomass conversion systems with 82 percent or higher efficiency, and industrial users who install electric motors with efficiency level 1. Such clear eligibility rules reduce program implementation costs, but, like other subsidy programs (such as tax credits), they do so by allowing free riders to benefit.

One expert distinguished three useful methods for establishing white-certificate rights:

1. The mass-default method, under which a technology by definition qualifies for white certificates.
2. The analytic method, under which the value of white certificates is based on on-site inspection of specific projects (which, given the high cost of such inspection is realistic only for large, mainly industrial projects).

3. Basing qualification on metered energy consumption reductions, which can be awarded only *ex post* (Grattieri, 2008).

Most of the white-certificate programs thus far have used the first method. In France, 95.4 percent of the certificates awarded have been in the residential sector.

Observations

White-certificate programs that mix sectors can be expensive to administer and, depending on the baseline case, can either reward investments that would have taken place anyway or require such large investments that they have limited uptake. Verification can also be an issue, especially in the case of the otherwise more cost-effective mass-default method. Commercial real estate may be sufficiently unique in terms of longevity of assets, diversity of building types, and financing and leasing characteristics to merit specifically tailored white-certificate/abatement programs such as Australia's Efficient Buildings Scheme.

Measuring Program Impact

Discussion

Another of the challenges in designing and implementing energy efficiency programs in commercial real estate is finding ways to evaluate the impact of policy initiatives. Questions related to energy efficiency in buildings policies include the following: Does the requirement that energy performance certificates be presented during real-estate transactions result in measurable pre-transaction investments in energy efficiency measures to improve the building's rating? What proportion of investments in buildings efficiency that earned white certificates would have happened without the incentive? Do high design-rated or performance-rated buildings obtain higher net rental returns or sales prices? What are the likely energy savings of proposed new measures?

The International Energy Agency and the United Nations Environment Program have prepared papers summarizing efforts that have been undertaken to evaluate the effectiveness of a variety of energy efficiency programs (Geller and Attali, 2005; Koeppel and Ürge-Vorsatz, 2007). Both organizations acknowledge that the central problem is how to measure with precision the impact of individual policies that are commonly implemented in packages. Among other problems are the challenges of establishing a valid business-as-usual base case, disaggregating information from price and incentive effects, and calculating "rebound" effects.[35] A review of studies performed for the U.S. Department of Energy found that the rebound effect for residential space heating and water heating averaged between 10 and 40 percent (Greening, Green, and Difiglio, 2000). In Austria, an analysis of residential building retrofits found a space-heating rebound effect of 20 to 30 percent (Haas and Biemayr, 2000), and in the UK, some 30 percent of potential energy savings from retrofit measures in the late 1990s was negated by low-income households that sought increased comfort (Milne and Boardman, 2000). In some cases, a rebound effect stems from an unintended consequence, as when better

---

[35] In buildings, the rebound effect occurs when improved insulation and other thermal efficiency improvement investments allow the same internal temperature to be maintained at a lower cost, but consumers respond by raising the temperature on the thermostat in winter or lowering it in summer, negating a proportion of the energy savings.

insulation causes heat to spread more widely (especially if doors are left open that were closed before).[36] In Germany, a study confirmed the existence of the split-incentive problem, as well as the positive effects of energy audits on behavior (Schleich, 2004).

The California Measurement Advisory Council, a joint venture supported by a group of California utilities, develops energy efficiency measurement protocols and has highlighted the special difficulty of calculating incremental-measure cost for energy efficiency measures included in new construction. In many cases, a base-case design is never developed, specified, or bid, and the cost of designed-in energy efficiency measures (cooling-equipment downsizing, fewer light fixtures, etc.) can be low or negative (Mahone, 2009).

Research in the United States has demonstrated the market value of voluntary energy ratings of both the design and use type. An analysis of microdata on 694 certified green (ENERGY STAR or LEED-rated) office buildings demonstrated that the green buildings obtained higher rents and maintained higher occupancy rates than did 7,489 comparable buildings located within a quarter mile radius of the green buildings. Rents for green office space were about 2 percent higher than rents for comparable certified buildings and, adjusted for the higher average occupancy rates, the "effective" rents were, on average, 6 percent higher (Eichholtz, Kok, and Quigley, 2008). A study of ENERGY STAR–rated office properties calculated that net incomes per square foot were 7 percent higher than those of comparable conventional properties (resulting from 11 percent lower utility expenditures, 5 percent higher rents, and 0.8 percent higher occupancy rates) (Pivo and Fisher, 2009).

In Denmark, a recent study examined the impact of energy performance labels on investment in energy savings. The study was based on consumer behavior following home sales transactions between 1999 and 2002, when energy labels were mandated for real-estate transactions under the Danish national scheme but the EPBD had not yet been adopted. Denmark has a comprehensive national registry of house sales, and the Danish Energy Authority tracks energy labels issued to specific properties. In addition, utilities provided the researchers with access to data on natural-gas usage by property address. Although the labels were mandated by domestic law, there were no significant penalties for noncompliance (which was fortuitous, from a research standpoint). The study did not consider house transaction prices, but rather sought to determine whether purchasers of single-family homes with labels (including recommendations for cost-effective investments) used less energy in the four years following the sale than did a control group that made purchases of houses without labels or certificates.

The Danish study found no significant energy savings attributable to the labeling scheme. Except during the first two years of ownership for A-labeled houses, there was no significant relationship between labeling and reduced energy use (the hypothesis had been that there would be a negative correlation between labeling and gas usage and that such an effect would be greatest in C-labeled homes, as these had the most cost-effective energy investment possibilities) (Kjaerbye, 2008).

In contrast, an Australian study demonstrated a clear impact of energy labeling on property valuation in the residential sector. The Australian Capital Territory has required mandatory disclosure of energy efficiency ratings (EERs) of residential properties since 1999. The EERs are calculated by trained assessors who use a thermal software package called FirstRate. The EERs, which use a star rating from 1 to 10 in half-star increments, must be disclosed in all

---

[36] Email from UK energy consultant, June 27, 2009.

advertising material, and the full certificate must be supplied at settlement. To gather data for the study, the researchers examined all Australian Capital Territory house sales data for 2005 and 2006. Relevant characteristics (floor space, lot area, lot location, window area, etc.) were described, and the effect of house price inflation was taken out. After hedonic analysis of the effects of the variables, the study concluded that EER ratings were positively associated with sales prices, with the increment for each half-star rating equivalent to 1.23 percent of the sales price in 2005, and 1.91 percent in 2006. Put another way, holding all other characteristics constant, a 0.5 increase of the EER star rating for a detached house with a median sales value of AU $365,000 in 2005 would increase the sales value by AU $4,489 (Department of the Environment, Water, Heritage and the Arts, Commonwealth of Australia, 2008).

An estimate of the *expected* impact of buildings energy efficiency measures was provided by the European Commission as part of its proposal for an EPBD recast (European Commission, 2008). As required under EU administrative procedures, the Commission examined the possible impacts, large and small, that could be expected to result from a variety of additional measures under consideration for the recast. On the basis of the Commission's analysis, some proposed measures were rejected because the cost-benefit ratio was insufficient, while others were rejected on political grounds, such as the assertion that they impinged on the EU principle of subsidiarity. The Commission's final assessment concluded that the four main measures in the recast[37] would be expected to save 60 to 80 million tons of oil-equivalent energy per year, which would be equal to 5 to 6 percent of total EU final energy demand in 2020 (European Commission, 2008). The Commission predicted such savings in part because of its judgment that the 2002 EPBD has not achieved its objectives. In particular, the Commission criticized the "low ambition in the implementation of the EPBD by the member states," noting that EPCs were of "very low quality," inspections of boilers and HVAC systems have had "limited impact," and energy performance requirements set by member states "do not fully meet expectation with regard to their level of ambition" (European Commission, 2008).

Observations

The public policy approaches of the EU and Australia for promoting energy efficiency in buildings are quite new or, in the case of the promised Australian national program and the proposed recast of the EPBD, even still under consideration. Thus, systematic analysis of the effects of the policies is not yet possible. There is, however, increasing international sharing of insights and information on buildings energy efficiency programs across the Atlantic and Pacific. The EU's Buildings Platform website, now restyled as Build-up: Energy Solutions for Better Buildings, provides a valuable service in linking buildings and energy professionals around the world and in disseminating new research. The Organisation for Economic Co-operation and Development and the International Energy Agency also play such a role.

---

[37] The four main measures are (1) abolishing the 1,000-sq-m floor-space minimum for requiring EPCs for renovation, (2) requiring member states to put in place quality-assurance and compliance systems to oversee issuance of energy performance certificates, (3) implementing more robust boiler and HVAC inspection systems, and (4) benchmarking national ratings schemes.

CHAPTER FIVE

Conclusions

Some 40 percent of the primary energy used in developed countries is used to heat, cool, and light buildings or is utilized within buildings. Estimates by the IPCC, analyses by McKinsey & Company, and other studies have noted opportunities to achieve substantial, relatively low-cost improvements in energy efficiency in commercial real estate. In recent years, the EU and its member nations and the Australian Commonwealth and some of its states and territories have pioneered public policies to promote energy efficiency in buildings. These policies are still in their development phases. The EU recently proposed amendments to its landmark 2002 EPBD that would remedy its inconsistent implementation and increase its impact. In Australia, buildings energy efficiency programs were first implemented by the states of New South Wales and Victoria and the Australian Capital Territory. The national government has made a commitment to implement a national energy efficiency program that includes a buildings component in 2010.

Implementation Issues

A number of issues have arisen in the implementation of buildings energy efficiency policies in the EU and Australia. These include

- Effects of building codes
- Use of energy performance certificates
- Promoting energy efficiency in public buildings
- Training and certification of experts
- Implementing white-certificate programs
- Measuring the impact of buildings energy efficiency programs.

Building Codes

Building codes are very effective in improving energy efficiency in buildings, because meeting their energy requirements is mandatory in all new construction and significant renovation, and the requirements are implemented by public bodies alongside safety provisions. By combining energy efficiency with safety provisions, the energy characteristics can often be obtained at low or minimal marginal cost. Unfortunately, as a public policy tool, building codes are slow to have an aggregate effect on energy use, because even in years of healthy economic growth, only about 3 percent of a nation's building stock is newly built or renovated. During a recession, the proportion is even lower. As codes get more complex and cover new areas, such as energy efficiency, ensuring effective enforcement becomes more of a challenge. A major decision in designing codes concerns whether they should be prescriptive or performance-based. Most codes are highly prescriptive, because their costs for assessment of compliance are low, and they allow building-materials manufacturers to standardize. The downside is that prescriptive codes can inhibit design innovation.

Energy Certificates

The requirement to present an appraisal of a building's energy characteristics on a certificate at the time of settlement of building transactions (such as sales or leases) is a central aspect of the EU's approach. Some Australian states and the Australian Capital Territory also require energy certificates. The logic behind requiring such certificates is that the information they present will cause buyers and sellers (or lessees and lessors) to value good energy performance. But in the case of sales, many other documents and disclosures are usually exchanged at the time of settlement, and at that point price is often agreed, which may reduce the impact of certificates on behavior. To make certificates more effective in influencing behavior, the EU's EPBD recast proposes to require energy ratings to be disclosed when properties are listed or advertised.

A second major issue associated with certificates is whether their ratings should be based on a building's energy efficiency design characteristics, its measured energy performance, or, as some jurisdictions have sought, both. The EU leaves this decision to the discretion of member states. A design-based approach is often the only alternative for new construction, and it facilitates cross-building comparisons. It also recognizes that building owners frequently have no control over tenant behavior. Energy-use ratings are based on measured energy use by a building or unit, can be prepared by a utility, and are more readily auditable.

A third issue concerns the selection of benchmark buildings or standardized rating levels to simplify the evaluation and comparison of rating data for consumers. On one hand, ratings designers want their ratings to reflect a high level of energy performance to realize the efficiency gains that are the goal of the public policy. On the other hand, attention may need to be paid to incentives for owners of older, poorly performing buildings. Sometimes the "low-hanging fruit" is the improvement of older buildings that are lower on the rating scale. If the top market-valued levels of energy efficiency are out of reach, there will be little incentive for efficiency improvement investment.

Research has demonstrated the existence of a rebound effect, where users respond to improved thermal efficiency with higher thermostat settings to improve their comfort at the same cost. Paradoxically, the impact of consumer behavior increases with higher building thermal efficiency (since the building leaks less energy). For this reason, rating and certificate systems based on measured energy use may work better for the residential sector than for the commercial sector.

Promoting Energy Efficiency in Public Buildings

In the EU, additional energy efficiency disclosure obligations are imposed on public buildings. Each member state can decide what constitutes a "public" building, but in countries to which the EPBD applies, public buildings must have DECs posted to inform visitors and occupants of their energy efficiency ratings. In Australia, several jurisdictions have policies that set a minimum Green Star rating for buildings that are leased or purchased. The market power of the state governments in Victoria and New South Wales is such that these policies are said to establish a de facto minimum for characteristics of new speculative office-space construction. A requirement to display energy certificates in prominent places (where voters can see them) can serve as an incentive for public authorities to invest in energy efficiency for publicly owned or leased buildings. Some EU member states, such as Germany, have achieved good results with display certificates. In others, however, implementation is new and partial. Some (particularly subnational) jurisdictions have resisted the potentially significant costs involved in obtaining the appraisal and rating of many dispersed public buildings, even before the cost of energy efficiency improvements is considered. Yet objective disclosure in such ubiquitous and much-visited structures as schools, post offices, and public-service offices could garner public support and understanding for capital improvement programs. Because the public sector normally has full control over its buildings (eliminating the split-incentive and privacy problems), it would generally be preferable that energy certificates for public buildings be based on actual energy usage rather than design criteria or should include both indicators.

Training and Certification of Experts

The credibility and effectiveness of energy efficiency public policies in the EU and Australia depend most of all on the quality and impartiality of the experts who review building designs, inspect completed buildings, and issue ratings certificates. Unlike mass-produced products, many buildings are unique or customized by location. Design and performance thus should ideally be based on case-by-case reviews of structures and their sites. In the European and Australian systems, ratings can add substantial market value to buildings—or can decrease value. It is therefore necessary to train and certify a relatively large number of experts to determine energy performance ratings and support white-certificate schemes. A further complication is that the largest number of inspectors is apt to be required at the initiation of a scheme, a time at which no building is certified. A shortage of trained experts in most member states led the EU to postpone the entry in force of the EPBD for three years, to January 1, 2009, but even as of April 2009, several member states did not have functioning certification programs, because they lacked sufficient trained and certified experts to implement them. The EU's EPBD recast will require adoption of a formal quality-assurance program, such as random checks, to maintain the credibility of the system. Other credibility issues concern the degree of independence of inspectors and their compensation model. Roughly half of the EU member states allow inspectors to be employees of interested parties (building design firms or developers, for example), merely requiring that inspections be carried out in an "independent manner." Care also needs to be given to incentives, since ratings can add substantial market value to buildings.

White-Certificate Programs

White-certificate programs are not per se public policy programs to improve energy efficiency in buildings. White certificates have come to mean tradable rights based on specified energy efficiency investments, which may include investments in improving the energy efficiency of buildings. White-certificate programs have been instituted as part of cap-and-trade programs in Australian states, and also in Italy and France. Two key challenges for white-certificate programs are defining "business as usual" (determining the reduction in energy use to be imposed on an obligated party—typically a utility) and verifying consumer behavior that qualifies for certificates. Under the GGAS white-certificate program in New South Wales, most of the certificates were earned by firms that distributed low-cost efficiency equipment (typically CFLs and low-flow shower heads) to building owners and aggregated the efficiency savings to earn and sell white certificates. Subsequent studies found a mixed record of installations. As a public policy approach to energy efficiency in buildings, therefore, white-certificate programs can provide incentives, but their effectiveness depends on the rigor of the efficiency gains required and the system of verification and enforcement. One Australian group is proposing adoption of a buildings-only white-certificate program in which efficiency improvement obligations are placed on owners in the office sector; the obligations can be met by investments in energy savings or by purchasing white certificates from other buildings that achieve better-than-required energy savings.

Measuring Program Impact

The EU and Australian buildings energy efficiency policies reviewed in this study are too new to allow their impact to be studied systematically. Moreover, it is difficult to disaggregate the effects of aspects of public policies that are customarily implemented in bundles (i.e., with pricing, tax incentives, and other components). One study of residential building transactions in Denmark could find no statistical relationship between energy use by households and the presentation of energy performance certificates at the time of sale. In contrast, a study in the Australian Capital Territory found a significant correlation between energy rating and sales price, after controlling for other factors. A study of the office-building market in the United States found that buildings with (voluntary) energy efficiency design that also used energy ratings achieved significantly higher rental income and lower vacancy rates, on average, than comparable buildings in close proximity. However, more research is required to assess accurately the cost-effectiveness of various policies for improving energy efficiency in buildings.

Lessons for the United States

The experiences of Europe and Australia suggest that effective policies to promote energy efficiency in buildings can be designed using information disclosure, building codes, financial incentives, and benchmarking. The rollout of such policies and their consistent implementation, however, pose special challenges. This preliminary review of the EU and Australian record suggests the following key insights that should be taken into account by U.S. policymakers as they consider analogous policy approaches:

- **Building codes.** In the near term, regional (climatic zone) consistency in the energy efficiency requirements for building codes would be highly desirable. This would allow building-materials manufacturers to improve and standardize building components. Given the importance of tenant behavior to energy consumption, consideration also should be given to applying energy efficiency code requirements to tenant interior space adaptations, especially in office and retail buildings. For the longer term, performance codes should be considered, but in the short term, simpler-to-administer prescriptive codes are preferable. Any expanded use of building codes should be accompanied by aggressive training and quality-assurance programs for inspectors.
- **Certificates.** An information mechanism such as EPCs needs to be simple enough to be understandable yet meaningful enough to affect marketplace behavior. Benchmarking can help, but the enormous variety of building types and siting makes establishment of reference grades very difficult. Once benchmark values are established, allowing (or, even

better, requiring) them to be used in property advertisements and listings seems preferable to requiring declarations at the time of settlement.

- **Incentives for improvements to existing buildings.** Public policies (especially building codes) affect the energy performance primarily of newly built structures. However, the key to achieving widespread energy efficiency gains in the buildings sector is making operational improvements and retrofitting existing buildings. Operational improvements can achieve significant savings at relatively low cost, and in the process, building managers become more aware of what needs retrofitting, and they become more demanding of retrofitting solutions. Benchmarks are an imperfect instrument for encouraging operational improvements because of the wide variety of existing buildings. Energy usage monitoring/incentives, marketable "white" abatement certificates, inspection, and improvement-recommendation systems will be equally critical.
- **Public buildings.** Buildings in the public sector should continue to be a test bed for new energy-saving ideas and should promote awareness of buildings energy performance levels. Nationwide standards for disclosure of energy performance of public buildings could serve both objectives. Given public sector control of most public building operations, disclosure should usually be based on measured energy usage, with an option to provide design ratings if they are available.
- **Training and certification of experts.** The credibility of any buildings energy efficiency program depends on the quality and impartiality of the experts who review designs and usage data. No certificate or rating program should be started until an adequate supply of trained and licensed inspectors is on hand. National standards for training and certification could reduce the burden on states.
- **White certificates.** The buildings sector, with its large potential energy efficiency gains, can be an important part of a carbon (or energy use) cap-and-trade program. The challenge will be to credibly evaluate energy performance improvements and to ensure the credibility of certificates in a sector with so many actors. In the United States, it would be more difficult for utilities to play the role of aggregator and verifier than it is in a country such as Australia, which has state-owned electricity monopolies. Establishment of a system of buildings efficiency ratings and the availability of a cadre of trained and licensed experts to implement it thus would seem to be a precondition for rollout of any broad-based white-certificate program in the United States.
- **Encouragement of voluntary measures.** A variety of voluntary buildings energy initiatives already exist, including voluntary rating schemes (ENERGY STAR, LEED, BREEM, and others), "green leases" (in the UK and Australia), and tenant energy statements (in the UK). National policy should continue to encourage these schemes, as they can lead to new approaches and can front-load the development of energy evaluation expertise in the private sector.
- **Monitoring and evaluation.** Effective systems for monitoring and evaluation will be needed to support public policy approaches to increasing efficiency in this varied, but important sector. Consideration should be given to increasing the building-energy-use research budgets of the EPA and the Department of Energy.

APPENDIX

List of Interviewees

Maria Atkinson, Lend Lease Corporation

Costa Balaras, Institute for Environmental Research and Sustainable Development, National Observatory of Athens

William Bordass, Usable Buildings Trust

Jonna Byskata, United Technologies

Hywell Davis, The Chartered Institution of Building Services Engineers

Martin Elsberger, Directorate General for Energy & Transport, European Commission

Zdrako Genchev, EnEffect/EcoEnergy

Stephen Grieg, Victoria Energy Efficiency Target

Adam Hinge, Sustainable Energy Partnerships

Anton Ivanov, Bulgaria Energy Forum

Richard Kauntze, British Council of Offices

Jean Lupinacci, ENERGY STAR, Environmental Protection Agency

Barry Lynham, Knauf Insulation

Romily Madew, Australian Green Business Council

Cliff Majersik, Institute for Market Transformation

Eduardo Maldonado, Engineering Department, University of Porto, Portugal

Peter Mihalos, DTZ Mihalos S.A.

Stratos Paradias, International Union of Property Owners

Stina Soewarta, European Commission

Adriana Spassova, EQE Bulgaria

Che Wall, Lincolne Scott

Andrew Warren, The European Alliance of Companies for Energy Efficiency in Buildings

References

Alliance to Save Energy, *Zero Energy Commercial Buildings Initiative*, Washington, D.C., April 2008. As of July 27, 2009:
http://www.ase.org/content/article/detail/4091

Andrews, Clinton J., and Uta Krogmann, "Technology Diffusion and Energy Intensity in U.S. Commercial Buildings;" *Energy Policy*, No. 37, 2009, p. 542.

Antinucci, Marcello, "Concerted Action, Annex 2: Inspection of Boilers and Air Conditioners: Supporting Transposition and Implementation of the Directive 2002/91/EC CA – EPBD (2005–2007)," European Commission, Intelligent Energy – Europe, Brussels, 2008.

Australian Sustainable Built Environment Council, *The Second Plank – Building a Low Carbon Economy with Energy Efficient Buildings*, n.d. As of July 24, 2009:
http://www.asbec.asn.au/files/ASBEC%20CCTG%20Second%20Plank%20Report%202.0_0.pdf

British Property Federation, *Landlord's Energy Statement, Tenant's Energy Review*, n.d. As of July 25, 2009:
http://www.les-ter.org/page/home

Commission of the European Communities, *Action Plan for Energy Efficiency in the European Community*, Brussels, 2000.

Creyts, J., A. Derkach, S. Nyquist, K. Ostrowski, and J. Stephenson, *Reducing U.S. Greenhouse Gas Emissions: How Much at What Cost?* McKinsey & Company, U.S. Greenhouse Gas Abatement Mapping Initiative Executive Report, December 2007. As of July 27, 2009:
http://www.mckinsey.com/clientservice/ccsi/pdf/US_ghg_final_report.pdf.

Crossley, David, "White Certificates in Australia," presented at CESI Ricerca Conference, Milan, October 22, 2008. As of July 27,2009:
http://www.efa.com.au/Library/David/Conference%20Papers/2008/WhiteCertificatesinAustralia.pdf

David, Hubert, "The 50 Years History Behind the EPBD: From the European Coal and Steel Community to the EPBD," *EPBD Buildings Platform*, 2007.

Demirbilek, F. N., U. Yalçiner, A. Ecevit, M. Inanici, and O. Demirbilek, "Energy Conscious Dwelling Design for Ankara," *Building and Environment*, Vol. 35, No. 1, 2000, pp. 33–40.

Department of the Environment, Water, Heritage and the Arts, Commonwealth of Australia, *Energy Efficiency Rating and House Price in the ACT*, Canberra, 2008.

Deringer, J., M. Iyer, and Y. J. Huang, "Transferred Just on Paper? Why Doesn't the Reality of Transferring/Adapting Energy Efficiency Codes and Standards Come Close to the Potential?" *Proceedings of the 2000 ACEEE Summer Study on Energy Efficiency in Buildings*, Pacific Grove, Calif., August 2004 (cited in Sonja Koeppel and Diana Ürge-Vorsatz, *Assessment of Policy Instruments for Reducing Greenhouse Gas Emissions from Buildings*, Report for the UNEP–Sustainable Buildings and Construction Initiative, UNEP and Central European University, Budapest, October 2007. As of August 10, 2009:
http://www.unep.fr/shared/publications/pdf/WEBx0126xPA-SBCIpolicyTool.pdf)

Eichholtz, P., N. Kok, and J. Quigley, *Doing Well by Doing Good*, Berkeley Program on Housing and Urban Policy, Berkeley, Calif.: University of California, Berkeley, Wo8-001, 2008.

Energy Information Administration, Commercial Buildings Energy Consumption Survey (CBECS), Washington, D.C.: Department of Energy, 2008. As of July 27, 2009:
http://www.eia.doe.gov/emeu/cbecs/cbecs2003/detailed_tables_2003/detailed_tables_2003.html/

European Commission, *Energy Performance of Buildings Directive*, Directive 2002/91/EC of the European Parliament, 2002.

———, *Green Paper on Energy Efficiency, Doing More with Less*, 2005. As of August 10, 2009:
http://ec.europa.eu/energy/efficiency/doc/2005_06_green_paper_book_en.pdf

———, *Proposal for a Recast of the Energy Performance of Buildings Directive Impact Assessment*, COM(2008)780(final), 2008.

Fisk, W. J., "Health and Productivity Gains from Better Indoor Environments and Their Implications for the U.S. Department of Energy," presented at E-Vision 2000 Conference, Washington, D.C., October 2000. As of July 27, 2009:
http://eetd.lbl.gov/IED/viaq/pubs/LBNL-47458.pdf

Geller, H., and S. Attali, *The Experience with Energy Efficiency Policies and Programmes in IEA Countries, Learning from the Critics*, Paris: International Energy Agency, 2005.

Grattieri, Walter, "Challenges in Energy Efficiency Investment," presented at IEA Seminar on White Certificates: The Italian Experiences Gained in Regulation, Monitoring, and Verification, Milan, October 22, 2008.

Greening, L. A., D. L. Green, and C. Difiglio, "Energy Efficiency and Consumption—The Rebound Effect—A Survey" *Energy Policy,* Vol. 28,No. 6-7, 2000, pp. 389–401.

GVA Grimley Ltd.,"From Green to Gold 2008," *GVA Grimley Research Bulletin*, London, 2008, p. 7.

Haas, R., and P. Biemayr, "The Rebound Effect for Space Heating: Empirical Evidence from Austria," *Energy Policy,* Vol. 28, No. 6-7, 2000, pp. 403–410.

Jensen, Ole, and Morten Hansen, "Development of a Second Generation Danish Energy Certificate Scheme—Danish Experience," *ECEEE Summer Study 2007,* European Council for an Energy Efficient Economy, La Colle sur Loup, France, June 2007.

Kjaerbye, V., "Does Energy Labelling on Residential Housing Cause Energy Savings?" AKF (Danish Institute of Governmental Research), Working Paper, 2008.

Koeppel, Sonja, and Diana Ürge-Vorsatz, *Assessment of Policy Instruments for Reducing Greenhouse Gas Emissions from Buildings*, Report for the UNEP–Sustainable Buildings and Construction Initiative, UNEP and Central European University, Budapest, October 2007.

Koomey, Jonathan G., et al., "Addressing Energy-Related Challenges for the U.S. Building Sector: Results from the Clean Energy Futures Study," *Energy Policy,* No. 29, 2001, p. 1218.

Lend Lease Corporation, Lincolne Scott, and Advanced Environmental, *Lessons from the European Union and Australia to Improve Building Efficiency and the Case for the Efficient Building Scheme*, February 2009.

———, *Mandatory Disclosure of Commercial Office Building Energy Efficiency*, response to Consultation Regulation Document, Australia, 2009, p. 27. As of July 27, 2009:
http://www.environment.gov.au/settlements/energyefficiency/buildings/submissions/pubs/lendlease.pdf

Levine, M., et al., "Residential and Commercial Buildings," in *Climate Change 2007: Mitigation,* Contribution of Working Group III to the Fourth Assessment Report of the Intergovernmental Panel on Climate Change, Cambridge, UK: Cambridge University Press, 2007, pp. 404–405.

Mahone, D., *Incremental Measure Costs in New Construction Programs: White Paper on Best Practices and Regulatory Issues*, Fair Lawn, N.J.: CALMAC, Study PGE0273.01, 2009.

Maldonado, Eduardo, Peter Wouters, and Aleksander Panek, "Concerted Action: Detailed Report on Certification, Supporting Transposition and Implementation of the Directive 2002/91/EC CA – EPBD (2005 – 2007)," European Commission, Intelligent Energy – Europe, Brussels, 2008.

———, "Concerted Action: Detailed Report on Training Requirements for Experts and Inspections, Supporting Transposition and Implementation of the Directive 2002/91/EC CA – EPBD (2005 – 2007)," European Commission, Intelligent Energy – Europe, Brussels, 2008.

McKinsey Global Institute, *Curbing Energy Demand Growth: The Energy Productivity Opportunity: Commercial Sector,* May 2007.

Milne, G., and B. Boardman, "Making Cold Homes Warmer: The Effect of Energy Efficiency Improvements in Low-Income Households," *Energy Policy,* Vol. 28, No. 6-7, 2000, pp. 411–424.

Organisation for Economic Co-operation and Development, Working Party on National Environmental Policy, *Case Studies on Policy Instruments for Environmentally Sustainable Buildings,* ENV/EPOC/WPNEP(2001)33/FINAL, Paris, June 2002a.

———, Working Party on National Environmental Policy, *Design of Sustainable Building Policies: Scope for Improvement and Barriers,* ENV/EPOC/WPNEP(2001)5/FINAL, Paris, June 2002b.

Pivo, G., and J. Fisher, "Investment Returns from Responsible Property Investments: Energy Efficient, Transit-Oriented and Urban Regeneration Office Properties in the U.S. from 1998–2007," Responsible Property Investing Center, Boston College, University of Arizona, Benecki Center for Real Estate Studies, and Indiana University, Working Paper WP-08-2, rev. 2009.

Schettler-Kohler, Horst P., *Implementation of the EPBD in Germany: Status and Future Planning,* European Commission, EPBD Buildings Platform, 2008.

Schleich, J., "Do Energy Audits Help Reduce Barriers to Energy Efficiency? An Empirical Analysis for Germany," *International Journal of Energy Technology and Policy,* Vol. 2, No. 3, 2004, pp. 226–239.

Shorrock, L. "Assessing the Effect of Grants for Home Energy Efficiency Improvements," in *Proceedings of the ECEEE Summer Study,* European Council for an Energy Efficient Economy, Cote d'Azur, France, 2001.

U.S. Department of Energy, *Buildings Energy Data Book,* Table 3.1.4, Washington, D.C., 2008.